New Focus on Success

Ausgabe Technik

Workbook

Inhalt

1 Prepositions

→ SB, Text, p. 6

Complete the descriptions of the photos with prepositions from the box.

| at |
| down |
| in (4x) |
| of (7x) |
| off |
| on (5x) |
| through |
| with |

There are three photos __on__ [1] page 6. The photo _____ [2] the left shows somebody snowboarding _____ [3] the Alps. He or she is going _____ [4] the side _____ [5] a mountain that is covered _____ [6] fresh snow. The picture _____ [7] the middle is _____ [8] a group _____ [9] people who are canoeing _____ [10] Canada. _____ [11] the background you can see some trees. The photo _____ [12] the right is the biggest _____ [13] the three. It shows four backpackers _____ [14] the top _____ [15] a mountain. One _____ [16] them has taken his backpack _____ [17] his back and has put it _____ [18] the ground. Two _____ [19] them are looking _____ [20] a map and the fourth is looking _____ [21] some binoculars.

2 Simple present

→ SB, Looking at grammar, p. 9

Use the elements to make complete sentences. Add any missing words. Be careful about negative sentences and questions.

1 Blue Sky / be / travel agency / Fulham

    _____

2 Blue Sky / not sell / ordinary package holidays

    _____

3 how many / people / work / travel agency?

    _____

4 it / not be / easy / find / IT specialists / London

    _____

5 Jasmin / not look after / customers / shop

    _____

6 Kate and Michael / often / argue / business

    _____

7 Michael / not expect / many replies / job ad

    _____

8 Michael / want / sell / holidays / website

    _____

9 The Kings / live / flat / above / shop

    _____

10 what / Joshua and Andrea + do / Blue Sky?

    _____

11 what kind / holiday / Blue Sky + sell?

    _____

12 why / Jasmin + work / such long hours?

    _____

3 Present continuous

→ SB, Looking at grammar, p. 10

Use the present continuous to say what the people in the illustrations are doing.

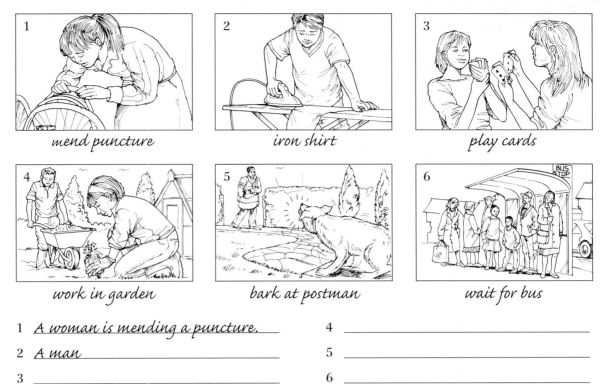

1 mend puncture

2 iron shirt

3 play cards

4 work in garden

5 bark at postman

6 wait for bus

1 _A woman is mending a puncture._   4 _____

2 _A man_ _____   5 _____

3 _____   6 _____

4 Simple present or present continuous?

→ SB, Looking at grammar, p. 9, p. 10

Cross out the incorrect verb form, simple present or present continuous.

1 Blue Sky *is looking*/~~looks~~ for web designers at the moment.
2 Kate and Michael *sometimes argue*/*are sometimes arguing* in front of customers.
3 Jasmin *is never leaving*/*never leaves* the office before 8 pm.
4 Andrea and Joshua *are talking*/*talk* to customers at present.
5 Andrea *normally takes*/*is normally taking* her lunch break at 12.30.
6 Joshua *is walking*/*walks* to work in summer.
7 Please be quiet. Kate *is speaking*/*speaks* on the phone.
8 Michael *attends*/*is attending* a meeting in Bristol all this week.
9 *Does Joshua live*/*Is Joshua living* with his parents at the moment?

5 Puzzle

Solve the puzzle to find the key word.

1 Other than rockets, ... are the fastest means of transport.
2 People travelling on a bus, say, are called '...'.
3 People who travel without a ... risk paying a big fine.
4 A word on page 9 that means 'Gepäck'.
5 Most tourists stay in a ... or a holiday apartment.
6 ... officers collect import duties on some goods.
7 A ... is a person or a book that gives you information about interesting places.
8 You only need one currency within the ... zone.
9 On holiday, a lot of people spend most of their time sunbathing on the ...

The key word is _____ .

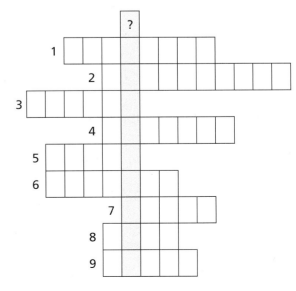

Unit **B** Where's my money? Refresher Course

1 John Barton

→ SB, Letter, p. 12   Link the sentence parts from A and B to make true statements about John Barton's holiday.

A
1 ~~John Barton booked an adventure holiday~~ *e*
2 At first, John was very satisfied with
3 But his problems started almost
4 Instead of staying in a pleasant hotel,
5 John nearly missed the rusty old minibus
6 Blue Sky's 'little village in the wilderness'
7 The Canadian guides advised the tourists
8 John wrote that hardly anything was

B
a as good as the catalogue said.
b as soon as he arrived in Winnipeg.
c Blue Sky's staff and service.
d he spent the night in a noisy motel.
e ~~in Canada through Blue Sky.~~
f that collected him from the motel.
g to contact Blue Sky about a rebate.
h was crowded with other tourists.

2 Describing a photo

→ SB, Ex. 1, p. 13   Complete the description of the photo on page 13 of the Student's Book with words from the box.

~~activity~~
bar
Catspaw
four-lane
furniture store
hotel
in German
John
on the edge of
open country
quiet place
vans
vehicles
Winnipeg

The photo is full of noisy *activity* [1], the same as the place John Barton stayed overnight in _____ [2]. The scene is obviously _____ [3] a larger town or city as you can see _____ [4] in the background. In the middle ground there is a _____ [5] rather like the motel that _____ [6] stayed at. Next door to the hotel there is a gambling casino called _____ [7], and after that there is a petrol station and a self-service _____ [8]. On the other side of the hotel there are some smaller businesses, including a _____ [9]. Traffic is quite heavy on the _____ [10] highway that runs past the hotel. In addition to cars, there are also several bigger _____ [11], such as campers and _____ [12]. In fact, this kind of road is called a 'Zubringer' _____ [13], and it is certainly not a _____ [14] to stay.

4 Refresher Course Unit B

3 Simple past

→ SB, Looking at grammar, p. 13

Use the simple past to complete the sentences with details from Michael's desk diary for part of last week.

Mon **10.05.02**	am/pm, interview web designers (+ Jasmin)
Tues **11.05.02**	10.30 am, bank, meeting 12.30 pm, meet Elli Snow of AmVac, lunch, Le Jardin 4.30 pm, take car for oil change (Ace Garages)
Weds **12.05.02**	11 am, visit architect, Queen's Square 3.30 pm, chair planning meeting, Canada project 7.30 pm, book concert tickets, Wigmore Hall
Thurs **13.05.02**	9 am, call Harry Potts (winter catalogue) 2.30 pm, collect Mother (City Airport) late afternoon, buy gift (Kate's birthday)

1 On Monday, Michael and Jasmin *interviewed* some web designers.

2 On Tuesday, Michael _____ at the _____ at _____ am.

3 At 12.30 pm, he _____ for _____ at _____ .

4 He _____ to Ace Garages _____ .

5 On Wednesday, Michael _____ .

6 He _____ about the _____ .

7 At _____ some _____ .

8 At 9 am on Thursday, _____ .

9 _____ .

10 _____ .

4 Simple past or past continuous?

SB, Looking at grammar, p. 13, p. 15

Cross out the wrong verb form.

A lucky break

Austrian mountain rescuers said yesterday that it *was / was being* [1] a miracle that an avalanche near Salzburg *did not kill / was not killing* [2] anybody. This *was / was being* [3] because the avalanche (Lawine) *came / was coming* [4] down the mountainside at about 1.15 pm, when many people *had / were having* [5] a break. Only a few people *were / were being* [6] on the slopes at the time, and they *skiied / were skiing* [7] well away from the path of the avalanche. However, about 30 skiers who *rested / were resting* [8] in a hut were trapped for several hours until rescuers *were able / were being able* [9] to reach them. In the valley, a number of cars that *went / were going* [10] to Salzburg when the avalanche *happened / was happening* [11] had to turn back. A car *ran / was running* [12] into another vehicle that *turned / was turning* [13] round in the middle of the road, but police *told / were telling* [14] reporters that that *was / was being* [15] the only accident that *took place / was taking place* [16].

Because of the blocked road, a woman who *expected / was expecting* [17] a baby did *not get / was not getting* [18] to the hospital in Salzburg in time. However, her husband *managed / was managing* [19] to reach a nearby farmhouse, and there the couple *had / were having* [20] some real luck. A doctor from Bochum *stayed / was staying* [21] at the house and he *helped / was helping* [22] to deliver the baby.

▆1▆ Susan Wood's holiday plans

→ SB, Text, p. 17/18

A Find the six false statements in the list and correct them. Look at the example first.

1 Susan Wood hopes to become a teacher after her gap year.
2 Susan wants to go abroad as soon as she leaves school.
3 She would like to go somewhere different such as India.
4 Susan's parents think that India or Africa would be best for their daughter.
5 Andrea isn't interested in how Susan will pay for her holiday.
6 Andrea tells Susan that some people pay their way by taking a temporary job.
7 Money is no problem because Susan's parents will pay all her costs.
8 Susan plans to come home as soon as her money runs out.
9 Andrea warns Susan that places like the Taj Mahal are very popular.
10 Susan came to Blue Sky just by chance.

1 _No, that is false/wrong. It says in the introduction that Susan_
  wants to be/become a nurse.

2 _The second statement is wrong, too. It says in the introduction_

_____

_____

_____

_____

_____

B How are these German sentences expressed in the dialogue? They are in the same order.

1 Was kann ich für Sie tun?

_____

2 Denken Sie an ein bestimmtes Reiseziel?

_____

_____

3 ... , aber das ist nicht das Entscheidende, oder?

_____

4 In dem Fall, haben Ihre Eltern recht.

_____

5 Wenn mein Geld alle ist, fahre ich einfach nach Hause.

_____

6 ... , aber ganz so einfach ist die Sache nicht.

_____

7 Eigentlich ist das der Grund, warum ich hier bin.

_____

2　The future

→ SB, Looking at grammar, p. 19

All the following future sentences are correct. Use the letters **A** to **F** to say why.

> A *will*-future, um eine Hoffnung auszudrücken
> B *will*-future, weil es sich um eine mit Sicherheit eintretende Voraussage handelt
> C *will*-future, um eine Vermutung zu äußern
> D *will*-future, um eine spontane Entscheidung auszudrücken
> E *going to*-future, weil es sich um eine Absicht handelt
> F *going to*-future, um ein voraussichtlich eintretendes Ereignis auszudrücken

1　Susan's parents hope that she'll choose a group holiday.　　　　　*A*

2　I don't think that Jasmin will leave Blue Sky now that she has an assistant.

3　Is it true that Michael is going to look for bigger offices?

4　You've missed your bus? Don't worry – I'll call a taxi.

5　Of course, you won't find European standards of comfort in the African bush.

6　I suppose Kate will spend less time in the shop now that we have more staff.

7　That woman says she is going to complain to Kate about Joshua's rudeness.

8　Don't go yet. It's going to rain any minute.

9　Goodbye, Kate. I'll see you at the meeting on Monday.

3　The future

→ SB, Looking at grammar, p. 19

Use the going to-future *(Pläne, Absichten)*, the present continuous with an adverb of future time *(zeitlich festgelegte Vorkehrungen bzw. Verabredungen)* or the simple present with future meaning *(fest terminierte, wiederkehrende Vorgänge)*.

1　Andrea (try) _____ to find an apartment in Fulham.

2　Blue Sky (move) _____ into new offices next September.

3　Hurry up. The bus (leave) _____ in a minute.

4　Joshua and Andrea (help) _____ Jasmin whenever they can.

5　Michael's plane (land) _____ at Gatwick at 10.15 am on Friday.

6　Ranjit (care) _____ for the children until Jasmin has more time.

7　The match (begin) _____ at 3.30 pm next Sunday.

8　The planning meeting (take place) _____ at 10 am tomorrow.

9　The tourists (arrive) _____ at the camp later today.

4　Tricky words

Cross out the wrong word to form correct sentences.

1　Jasmin is very *happy/~~lucky~~* at Blue Sky.
2　Always get a *receipt/recipe* for cash payments, OK?
3　Michael is going to *make/take* some photos of the new offices.
4　Football is by far the most popular *game/play* in the world.
5　Please *remember/remind* me to collect Kate from Heathrow this afternoon.
6　Why don't you get up? It's not healthy to *lay/lie* around all day.
7　Would you believe it? The train crashed because of just one *lose/loose* screw.
8　It's obvious that small cars are more *economic/economical* than big ones.
9　Have you *done/made* those letters yet, Michael?
10　Can you *say/tell* me the way to the nearest tube station, please?
11　Andrea's a very *sociable/social* person. She loves parties.
12　In Britain, you can *become/get* stamps at a lot of shops.

Unit D Honesty is best

1 A new policy

→ SB, Text, p. 21

Use the sentence elements to ask the questions that produced the answers below.
You must add some words.

1 – Blue Sky + introduce / its "Honesty is Best" policy

Why *did Blue Sky introduce its "Honesty is Best" policy* _____ ?
– Because of all the bad publicity about John Barton's holiday.

2 – Kings + start / their travel agency

Where _____ ?
– In Fulham in London.

3 – branches / company + have / today

How many _____ ?
– Fifteen nationwide.

4 – radio programme + describe / its listeners

What _____ ?
– The troubles of John Barton from Abingdon.

5 – John Barton + feel / misled / Blue Sky

Why _____ ?
– Because of the wrong information in the catalogue.

6 – support / Blue Sky / radio programme

Who _____ ?
– A girl called Susan Wood.

7 – Susan + read / Blue Sky's / "Honesty is Best" policy

_____ ?
– On the company's website.

8 – Blue Sky + react / bad publicity

How _____ ?
– Very quickly.

2 Synonyms

→ SB, Advertisement, p. 21

Find words of the same or nearly the same meaning in *the advertisement* for the following
words or expressions. They are in the same order.

1 only   *just* _____   7 excitingly different _____

2 largest   _____   8 destinations   _____

3 all over the country _____   9 very well-known   _____

4 prize-winning   _____   10 heaven   _____

5 more than   _____   11 journey   _____

6 chosen   _____   12 exaggerated claims   _____

3 Vocabulary: expressions

SB, Press report, p. 21

Complete the expressions from *the press report* with a verb from the box.

| call |
| complain |
| describe |
| disagree |
| feel |
| have |
| earn |
| react |
| read |
| ring |
| sell |
| support |

1 to *describe* somebody's problems

2 to _____ somebody a holiday

3 to _____ one thing something else

4 to _____ about misleading information

5 to _____ with somebody's complaints

6 to _____ a phone-in programme

7 to _____ somebody in an argument

8 to _____ about something on the internet

9 to _____ safe in somebody's hands

10 to _____ a nasty surprise

11 to _____ from a bad experience

12 to _____ to a situation

4 Describing graphs

Complete the description of the graph by crossing out the incorrect or less suitable adjective or adverb.

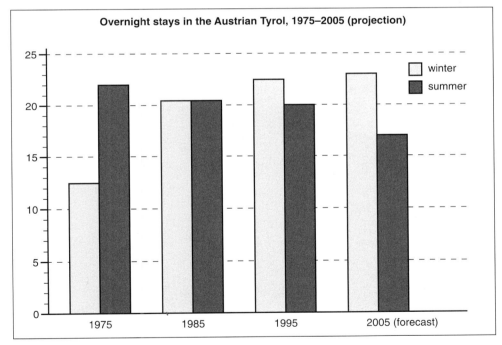

Overnight stays in the Austrian Tyrol, 1975–2005 (projection)

The graph above shows the *actual/~~possible~~* [1] overnight stays in the Austrian Tyrol during the summer *(dark/light* [2] grey) and winter *(dark/light* [3] grey) holiday seasons of 1975, 1985 and 1995, and the *projected/real* [4] figures for 2005.

The most *obvious/probable* [5] development during these years is that the winter has overtaken the summer as the Tyrol's *longest/most important* [6] holiday season. Hence, in 1975, there were *exactly/nearly* [7] twice as *many/much* [8] stays in summer as in winter. Ten years *after/later* [9], in 1985, the *forecast/recorded* [10] numbers of summer and winter stays were *different/equal* [11]. Then, during the *late/old* [12] 1980s and *early/first* [13] 1990s, a *big/strong* [14] change took place: the winter overtook the summer. And this development will *certainly/perhaps* [15] continue and *almost/even* [16] increase in the new millenium.

1 Some/any

→ SB, Looking at grammar, p. 29

Cross out the incorrect word.

1 Jasmin, could you give me ~~any~~/*some* help, please?
2 – Do you have *any*/*some* recordable CDs for Apple computers?
  – Of course. They are the same as CDs for *any*/*some* other computer.
3 There are *any*/*some* car parks in Chelsea, but there isn't *any*/*some* parking nearer our offices, I'm afraid.
4 – Can I get *any*/*some* A4-paper from the stationery cupboard, Kate?
  – Of course. Just take *any*/*some*. There's no need to ask.
5 Michael doesn't have *any*/*some* appointments this afternoon, but he must make *any*/*some* important phone calls.
6 – Have you had *any*/*some* luck finding an apartment yet?
  – No, but there are *any*/*some* interesting ads in the paper today. Perhaps I'll have *any*/*some* luck with them.
7 – Would you like *any*/*some* chips?
  – No, thanks. I never eat *any*/*some* fried food.
8 – Are there *any*/*some* replies to our job ad on the website, Jasmin?
  – Well, yes, but *any*/*some* of them are just a joke. That's the trouble with Jobs@ buttons. *Any*/*Some* people just don't take them seriously.

2 Some/any and compounds

→ SB, Looking at grammar, p. 29

Fill in **some, any** or one of the compounds **somebody/anybody, something/anything** or **somewhere/anywhere**.

1 – Listen, Kate! I think I heard __somebody__ downstairs in the shop.
  – Well, of course you heard __somebody__ . Jasmin's repairing __something__ on one of the computers.
2 – I can't find my car keys. Have you see them __anywhere__ ?
  – Yes, I think I saw them __some__ . Oh, yes – in the kitchen.
3 – I hope you didn't forget to buy _____ to drink.
  – Well, I bought _____ mineral water, but I suppose you mean _____ alcoholic, don't you
4 – Is there _____ good on TV tonight?
  – What a question! There's never _____ good on TV.
  – Oh, come on. I've seen _____ really good programmes lately.
5 – I'm looking for _____ statistics on camping holidays in Europe. Have you _____ idea where I could find some?
  – How about the internet? I'm sure you'll find _____ there.
6 – Do you know _____ about pub opening times in Berlin?
  – Sure. The short answer is that there aren't _____ . Pubs can open and close _____ time they like in Berlin, but I know there are stricter rules in _____ other German states.

3　Much, many, a lot of, plenty of

→ SB, Looking at grammar, p. 30

Fill in **much, many, a lot of** or **plenty of**.

1　I don't have ___much___ time now, Michael. There are ___many___ customers in the shop.

2　Why on earth did you buy so ___a lot of___ bread? You know that we have ___many___

   rolls left over from the party. No wonder we throw away so ___much___ food.

3　– How ___much___ holidays have we sold this month?

   – 122 so far, and that's ___much___ more than we were expecting. People are showing

   ___much___ interest in eastern Europe at the moment.

4　– We are losing ___many___ customers because people have to wait too long.

   – Don't tell me. Do you have an idea how ___many___ complaints I have each week?

5　– How ___many___ replies have we had to our internet job ad, Jasmin?

   – Not _____ , I'm afraid, and _____ them are useless.

4　A little, a few

→ SB, Looking at grammar, p. 31

Fill in **little/a little, few/a few**.

1　We only had _____ customers this afternoon, so Joshua and Andrea could give

   Jasmin _____ help.

2　– Unfortunately, some successful men have ___little___ time for their children.

   – And what about working mothers? People should give them _____ thought.

3　– You know that doctors say you should only put ___little___ salt on your food.

   – Sure, but _____ of the doctors I know take their own advice.

4　– I only have _____ cash. What about you?

   – I only have _____ pounds. We'll have to pay by credit card.

5　There's _____ point in advertising if we can't handle the business it creates.

6　Could you wait a moment, please? I'll only be _____ minutes.

5　A crossword

→ SB, Text, p. 26

Complete the crossword with the missing words from the sentences. What is the hidden word?

1　Pils is a very popular kind of … .
2　At a … guests fetch food themselves
　 from tables.
3　Ben Nelson runs a party … for
　 business events.
4　Ben … Kate to choose a set buffet.
5　The meat of a pig is called … .
6　Kate is expecting 150 … in all.
7　If you keep … out of water too long,
　 they die.
8　The security guards will …
　 everybody coming into the building.
9　… is an alcoholic drink made from
　 grapes.

The missing word is _____ .

1 Advertising and us

1 Advertising media

→ SB, Focus, p. 32

Find the words in the anagrams to label the types of advert.

hipsorsnops
singritdave
tosper
dario moccermail
burrosech
none sings
fissaclide sad

_____ _____ _____

*n*_____*s*_____ _____ _____

2 Words: verbs and nouns

→ SB, Text B, p. 36

A Copy and complete the tables with words from the text.

Verb	Noun	Verb	Noun
attend	*attention*	_____	sale
produce	_____	_____	success
compete	_____	_____	introduction
manufacture	_____	_____	meaning

B Use pairs of words from **2A** to complete the following. (You may need to change forms of words slightly.)

1 Without advertising industry would _____ fewer goods, and the

_____ themselves would be more expensive.

2 Advertising increases _____ between producers, and because they have

to _____ with each other the price of goods is held down.

3 When a company _____ a new product in the market, it is very important

that its _____ is planned very carefully and given the right support.

4 Whether or not a new product _____ and becomes popular depends on

the _____ of the advertising campaign and the quality of the product.

5 With less advertising, companies _____ fewer products, and reduced

_____ hurt the future development of any business.

3 Comparison of adjectives

A Complete the list of adjectives – one formed from each noun in the table. Use your dictionary if necessary.

	Star 2	Traveller 1.4	FX5	
cost	***	**	*	*cheap/expensive*
appearance	**	*	***	*nice/ordinary looking*
speed	**	*	***	*fast*
age	***	**	*	*old*
economy	***	**	*	
reliability	*	***	**	
safety	**	***	*	
practicality	**	***	*	
comfort	**	***	*	
excitement	**	*	***	

B Ian needs a car for his band. He is looking at these cars and at the table in A above. Complete what he says using the adjectives in brackets (*** = best, * = worst).

'Well, of course the FX5 is (fast) _the fastest_ [1] and (exciting) _____

_____ [2] of them all, and it's (nice looking) _____ [3], too. The

trouble is that it's also (expensive) _____ [4] the others, and I haven't got

much money. I definitely need something which isn't (expensive) _____ [5] the

FX5, and I also need something which is (practical) _____ [6] for my

purposes. You see, I'm in a band, and I have to take my drums to gigs most weekends. The

answer has to be the Traveller 1.4. I know it isn't (new) _____ [7] the FX5 and it's

(slow) _____ [8] both the others, but it's certainly (practical) _____

_____ [9] of the three. It can carry the whole band and all our equipment, too. It

isn't (economical) _____ [10] the Star 2, I know, but the other band members

can help pay for petrol, so that's all right. It's important that it's (safe) _____ [11] and

(reliable) _____ [12] the others, and that it's also (comfortable)

_____ [13] of all three. I certainly wouldn't want anything (old)

_____ [14] the Star 2. It would probably fall to pieces in a few weeks!'

4 Comparison of adverbs

→ SB, Looking at grammar, p. 37/8

Next weekend, the band has to travel farther than ever before, and Ian wants to share the driving – but who with? Complete the paragraph using the correct adverbial forms of the adjectives in brackets.

He knows that Sue drives (safe) _____ [1] and (careful) _____ [2] of them all, but she also goes (slow) _____ [3] of all. Chris, on the other hand, drives (fast) _____ [4] Sue and, in fact, he drives (fast) _____ [5] of everybody in the band. Ian and Sue both think that he also drives (dangerous) _____ [6] of them all, too. He hasn't yet had a bad accident, but the police have stopped him for speeding (frequent) _____ [7] everybody else put together. No, Ian feels that he needs somebody who drives (quick) _____ [8] Sue but (careless) _____ _____ [9] and (dangerous) _____ [10] Chris. And of course, there's really only one person to ask: Bill. He is older than the rest of them and so has driven (long) _____ [11] anybody else, and Ian feels that he drives much (good) _____ [12] most other people on the road.

5 Plastic Coating Helps Ships Live Longer

→ SB, Technical reading, p. 40

Replace the underlined word or expression with a technical term from the press report. They are in the same order.

1 In industry, <u>mixtures</u> _____ of metals or metals and chemicals are often used instead of pure metals.

2 Ormecon says that polyaniline largely <u>gets rid of</u> _____ rust.

3 Polyaniline does not just <u>separate</u> _____ steel surfaces from moisture; it takes part in the rusting <u>activity</u> _____ .

4 The polyaniline coating <u>takes</u> _____ electrons from steel and <u>gives</u> _____ them to oxygen.

5 The chemical reaction <u>makes</u> _____ a coating of pure <u>rust</u> _____ .

6 The <u>big metal boxes</u> _____ used on ships rust very quickly in sea-water.

7 The <u>working</u> _____ life of steel <u>things</u> _____ is usually longer than that of paint.

8 In <u>tests outside the lab</u> _____ , polyaniline was much more <u>long-lived</u> _____ than zinc, for example.

9 With a polyaniline coating, containers never need <u>painting again</u> _____ .

10 Another big <u>plus</u> _____ is that polyaniline is much easier <u>to put on</u> _____ than zinc.

1 Words: workers

→ SB, Focus, p. 41

A Find job titles in the anagrams, and use them to label the things they work with.

> *gophartephor* ▪ *marf werrok* ▪ *critniaclee* ▪ *posh sastintas* ▪ *torac* ▪ *wistares* ▪
> *suner* ▪ *hancemic* ▪ *sentifs reniart* ▪ *sidrarehers* ▪ ~~*tenparcer*~~ ▪ *lalc treenc repootar* ▪
> *dearcroot* ▪ *hectare* ▪ *rerac* ▪ *knab krelc*

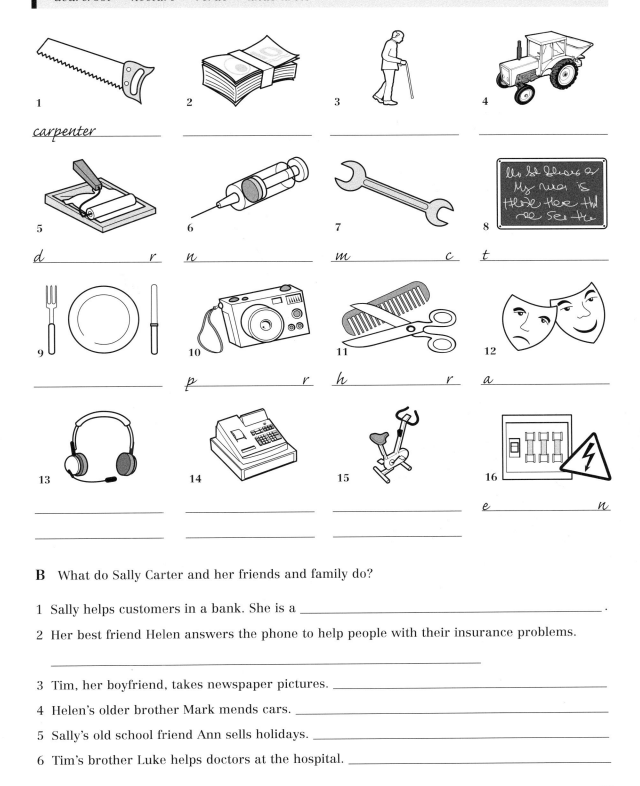

1 _carpenter_

2 _____

3 _____

4 _____

5 _d_____r_

6 _n_____

7 _m_____c_

8 _t_____

9 _____

10 _p_____r_

11 _h_____r_

12 _a_____

13 _____
   _____

14 _____
   _____

15 _____
   _____

16 _e_____n_

B What do Sally Carter and her friends and family do?

1 Sally helps customers in a bank. She is a _____ .

2 Her best friend Helen answers the phone to help people with their insurance problems.

_____

3 Tim, her boyfriend, takes newspaper pictures. _____

4 Helen's older brother Mark mends cars. _____

5 Sally's old school friend Ann sells holidays. _____

6 Tim's brother Luke helps doctors at the hospital. _____

2 Words: expressions with adverbs and prepositions

Complete the underlined expressions with an adverb or preposition from the list.

after
at
by
for
from
in
of
on

Shona has decided to become a full-time mum instead _____ [1] continuing her career. _____ first [2], after her first child was born, she thought she could continue to work. And she has tried hard to continue. _____ fact [3], she has tried desperately hard. She has also had quite a lot of help, _____ course [4], but _____ the end [5], it has just become too much for her. _____ example [6], she has become very upset by her daughter's sadness every morning when she takes her to playschool _____ the way [7] to work. And apart _____ [8] all the worries about her responsibilities as a mother, she has become terribly tired all the time. _____ all [9], she has been trying to do two full-time jobs for a long time. _____ chance [10], she and her husband Mark saw a TV discussion about the problem at the weekend and this helped her to decide to stop.

3 Simple past and present perfect

→ SB, Looking at grammar, p. 47

Compare the life of Elsie Hill (1885–1955) with events in the lives of her great-granddaughters, Sophie, Flora, Bianca, Julie and Lucy. Use the simple past and the present perfect.

Elsie	Age 5	almost (die) of measles (*Masern*)
	Age 13	(leave) school (find) / job, working at / local greengrocer's
	Age 18	(get) engaged to Edward Hill, / bicycle mechanic (marry) him / end of / year
	Age 19	(become) pregnant (stop) work
	Age 28	(have) / last of her three children

Sophie	Age 5	(have) her second vaccination (*Impfung*) against measles
Flora	Age 13	(begin) preparing for her first school exams
Bianca	Age 18	(leave) school · (take) / gap year before college, working in Chile
Julie	Age 19	(complete) / Business Studies course at / local college · (start) first job, working as / trainee supermarket manager
Lucy	Age 28	(marry) her long-term partner, Jake (have) her first child, but / (continue) her career in marketing

1 At the age of five, Elsie almost _____ .

At the same age, Sophie has just _____ .

2 When she was 13, Elsie _____ , and she _____ .

At the same age, Flora has recently _____ .

3 At the age of 18, Elsie _____ , and she _____

_____ .

At the same age, Bianca has just _____ , and she _____

_____ .

4 At the age of 19, Elsie _____ ,and she _____ .

At the same age, Julie has recently _____

and she _____ .

5 At the age of 28, Elsie _____ .

At the same age, Lucy _____ , and she

_____ , but _____ .

→ SB, Looking at grammar, p. 47

4 Simple past and present perfect continuous

The three mothers of Sophie and the others are talking about their daughters at a family party. Use the simple past or present perfect continuous.

Mum 1   how / Sophie / (enjoy) / first term / school

_____?

Mum 2   / (cry) / first day, but since then / (have) / great time

_____?

Mum 3   where / Bianca / (stay) since / (arrive) / Chile

_____?

Mum 1   / (stay) with / organization helping young, homeless children / Santiago

_____?

Mum 2   and how / Julie / (get on) / her new supermarket job

_____?

Mum 3   / (not like) / much at first, but recently / (have) / a much better time

_____?

Mum 1   and / Flora / (find) her new work for her GCSE exams all right

_____?

Mum 2   all / extra work (be) / shock at first, but we think / (manage) just fine recently

_____?

Mum 3   how / Lucy / (get on) / her new baby

_____?

Mum 1   / (find) it hard when / (start) work again, but / (deal) with all the problems well

_____?

5 What is 'energy'?

→ SB, Technical reading, p. 49

Complete the photo descriptions with words from the text.

Four photos are used to illustrate kinds of _____ [1]. In the first photo, you can

see a lighthouse in a stormy _____ [2]. Big _____ [3] are

breaking all around it. This illustrates the _____ [4] energy released by

_____ [5] sea and wind. The second photo shows some _____ [6],

which are used to store _____ [7] energy. In the third photo, the

_____ [8] of the sun are shining through the trees in a forest. This is a good

illustration of _____ [9] energy in the _____ [10]. The fourth

photo shows a _____ [11] that is holding back water in a _____ [12].

The _____ [13] energy in the weight of water is _____ [14] into

kinetic energy to drive a _____ [15] by gravitational _____ [16].

1 Words: opposites with prefixes

→ SB, Focus, p. 50;
Text A, p. 51;
Lernhilfen, p. 179, 180

Add the opposites of these words to the table. Use your dictionary if necessary.

> *ability ▪ accurate ▪ agree ▪ appear ▪ correct ▪ dependent ▪ direct ▪ efficient ▪*
> *employment ▪ expensive ▪ happy ▪ ~~healthy~~ ▪ honest ▪ legal ▪ like ▪ mature ▪*
> *natural ▪ perfect ▪ responsible ▪ rational ▪ regular ▪ satisfaction ▪ skilled ▪ usual*

un-	in-	*il-/im-/ir-	dis-
unhealthy			

*NB These are the same as *in-* but are used before words beginning with *l* (for *il-*) *m* or *p* (for *im-*)
and *r* (for *ir-*).

2 Words: definitions

→ SB, Text B, p. 54

Read the definitions and find words with the same meaning in the text. (They are in the same order.)

1 the condition of one's body (or mind), good or bad _____

2 immoral or illegal action that causes public shock and anger _____

3 to fight for what one believes in, often through the media _____

4 the getting of food from the land using no man-made chemicals _____

5 the getting of food from the land using mass-production techniques _____

6 place where wild animals and plants naturally live _____

7 animals kept on a farm _____

8 to sell at a lower price than others _____

9 businesses fighting each other for the same customers _____

3 Diet or not? must, mustn't, needn't

→ SB, Looking at grammar, p. 55

Use **must/mustn't** or **needn't** and the verbs in brackets.

LYN   I put on so much weight on holiday last week! I really

(go) _____ ¹ on a diet right now.

MUM   No, no, you (worry) _____ ². You look

fine. In fact, I worry that you eat too little, and you

certainly (do) _____ ³ that. You don't

want to become anorexic, do you?

LYN   Mum, you (be) _____ ⁴ mad! I'm certainly not going to do that!

MUM   Well, no, I was just joking. But I just mean you (even think) _____

_____ ⁵ about going on a diet. You look just right as you are.

LYN   Mum, you (keep) _____ ⁶ telling me what to do. I'm 18 now,

and you (stop) _____ ⁷ treating me like a kid!

MUM   All right, all right, you (get) _____ ⁸ angry. I'm not saying you

(go) _____ ⁹ on a diet. I'm just advising you that you

(do) _____ ¹⁰ that because you simply aren't overweight. OK?

LYN   OK. Sorry, Mum.

4 First aid: modal verbs

→ SB, Looking at grammar, p. 55

Dave Stockman runs a popular first aid class at the Sports and Leisure Centre. Translate the German to complete the talk.

Introduction

This week, we're looking at first aid on the road, and first, let me ask how many of you carry a first aid kit in your car. Hands up! So ... just five out of fifteen. Well, let me say this: even though the law doesn't say we *(müssen + carry)* _____ ¹ a kit, and so of course we *(nicht brauchen + do)* _____ ² so, it's still something we all *(sollten + do)* _____ ³. After all, a crash *(können + happen)* _____ ⁴ at any time on the road. So we really *(müssen + be)* _____ ⁵ ready for it – and know what we *(sollen + do)* _____ ⁶.

First things first

The first action you really *(müssen + take)* _____ ⁷ is warn other traffic – or else more vehicles *(könnten + crash)* _____ ⁸ into the ones already there. Secondly, to reduce the danger of fire, you *(müssen + switch off)* _____ ⁹ any engines that are still on. Thirdly, petrol *(könnten + escape)* _____ ¹⁰ from petrol tanks, so you *(nicht dürfen + let)* _____ ¹¹ anybody smoke near the crash.

If anybody is hurt, you *(müssen + call)* _____ ¹² an ambulance as fast as possible. If anybody there has a mobile, you *(können + ask)* _____ ¹³ them to make the call. They *(sollen + say)* _____ ¹⁴ exactly where the crash has happened and the numbers of vehicles and people in the crash.

First aid

Now for the first aid. First, you *(nicht sollen + move)* _____ [15] somebody who is hurt and still in a vehicle if there is no further danger. This is because you *(können + cause)* _____ [16] further injury. In other words, if you *(nicht müssen + move)* _____ [17] somebody, then don't.

If somebody has stopped breathing, first you *(sollen + move)* _____ _____ [18] the head backwards, and this *(können + help)* _____ _____ [19] breathing to start again. If it doesn't, then use mouth-to-mouth resuscitation *(Mund-zu-Mund-Beatmung)* until the person *(können + breathe)* _____ [20] again without help.

The casualty *(könnten + be)* _____ [21] in a state of shock and if so, you *(müssen + try)* _____ [22] to reduce this. You *(können + help)* to _____ [23] do this by keeping the person warm, by avoiding unnecessary movement, by staying with him or her and by talking positively.

One thing you *(nicht dürfen + do)* _____ [24] is to give the casualty anything to drink. This is because an operation with an anaesthetic *(könnten + be)* _____ [25] and *(nicht können + be done)* _____ [26] except on an empty stomach.

(Based on *The Highway Code: First Aid on the Road*, HMSO)

5 Weighty problems

→ SB, Technical reading, p. 58

Read the text and work out your normal healthy weight (nhw), your ideal healthy weight (ihw) and your body mass index (bmi). Use your own height and weight.

> You can easily calculate your normal healthy weight (nhw) in kilos by simply subtracting 100 from your height in centimetres, ie h(cm) – 100 = nhw. If you want to go further, subtract 10% from your nhw to find out your ideal healthy weight (ihw), ie h(cm) – 100 – 10% = ihw. However, this is only a very rough guide as it leaves out three important factors, ie age, sex and build (*Körperbau*).
> A more accurate – though still not perfect – guide is to work out your body mass index (bmi). To do this, take your weight in kilos and divide it by your height squared, ie $w(kg) \div h(m)^2$.
> Then round the answer up or down to the nearest whole unit.
> For example, Joshua Snow weighs 79 kg and is 1.82 m tall. Hence his calculation is as follows:
> $79 \div 1.82^2 = 79 \div 3.31 = 23.87 = 24$ bmi, which makes Joshua just normal according to the table below.
>
> | bmi | category |
> |---|---|
> | below 20 | underweight |
> | 20 – 25 | normal weight |
> | 26 – 30 | overweight |
> | over 30 | obese |

My normal healthy weight: h(cm) _____ – 100 = _____ nhw

My ideal healthy weight: h(cm) _____ – 100 = _____ – 10% = _____ ihw

My body mass index: w(kg) _____ $\div$ h(m)^2 _____ = _____

[h(m)^2 = _____ € _____ = _____]

Can't stop communicating!

1 Word field: Hi-tech

→ SB, Text A, p. 60 | **A** Find 16 'hi-tech' words (*senkrecht oder waagerecht*) from the text in the word square.

f	t	w	e	q	u	i	p	m	e	n	t	p	o	z	t	i	n	m	b	v
e	p	o	b	v	f	r	d	e	c	d	x	s	s	c	a	n	m	i	h	g
l	b	i	n	t	e	l	l	i	g	e	n	t	m	g	f	t	v	n	c	x
e	l	b	f	a	k	m	t	r	o	u	z	e	v	d	c	e	b	v	w	s
c	b	p	r	o	t	o	t	y	p	e	b	c	r	e	q	r	b	e	k	a
t	g	r	l	j	g	v	n	t	q	o	v	h	v	t	s	n	x	n	d	t
r	p	o	k	s	e	n	s	o	r	f	q	n	b	e	v	e	s	t	r	e
o	b	g	e	u	b	v	i	u	s	c	d	o	n	c	x	t	x	i	h	l
n	t	r	e	c	e	i	v	e	r	c	y	l	j	t	v	e	p	o	c	l
i	d	a	m	b	t	c	p	l	w	d	x	o	n	b	x	s	f	n	c	i
c	b	m	i	n	i	a	t	u	r	e	v	g	c	d	p	o	b	v	y	t
z	g	d	j	h	s	l	u	b	r	c	u	y	m	l	a	s	e	r	p	e
m	l	a	b	o	r	a	t	o	r	y	k	l	t	v	r	w	c	s	p	b

B Now complete the following with words from **1A**.

1 This _____ is the latest in anti-virus software.

2 All the computer _____ we bought two years ago is out of date.

3 This _____ is so powerful it can cut through a heavy steel door.

4 We've finished testing the RX300 _____ and hope to start production in time for the Christmas market.

5 The _____ of the microchip opened the way to modern computers.

6 Our new robot house cleaner uses 22 different _____ to guide it.

2 Words: opposites

→ SB, Text B, p. 63 | **A** Find opposites of the following in the letters to the editor.

Letter 1

| sold | _____ | delight | _____ | the opposite | _____ |

Letter 2

| the last | _____ | allow | _____ | with difficulty | _____ |

Letter 3

| the next | _____ | despair | _____ | modern | _____ |

Letter 4

| similar to | _____ | succeed | _____ | lose | _____ |
| destroy | _____ | defend | _____ | true | _____ |

B Use pairs of opposites from **2A** to complete the following.

1 During _____ ten years, internet use has increased beyond belief, but

will it go on growing like this during _____ ten years?

2 Young people learn to use new technology quickly and _____ , but older people often

do so only _____ .

3 _____ technology gives ordinary people a freedom to communicate globally

that was never possible with _____ media.

4 Some governments do not want to _____ their people free speech through

internet use, but it is very hard for them to _____ it.

5 Not every new 'hi-tech' product _____ and becomes popular. Many _____

and are quickly forgotten.

6 When I _____ my new computer, I _____ my old one, but I didn't get much for it.

→ SB, Looking at
grammar, p. 64

3 Relative clauses: which/that and who/that

Match the websites to the sentence parts in the boxes. Write out the complete sentences
adding necessary relative pronouns.

Box 1 *which/that*	Box 2 *who/that*
carries masses of data for football fans	need advice about their holiday
lists lots of travel suggestions for people	arrangements
gives details of many mobiles to help	love shopping
people	are getting married
provides a lot of ideas and help for	are interested in British clubs and
women	players
has lots of information for couples	are trying to decide which one to buy

1 www.all-about-weddings.co.uk

This is a site _____

_____

2 www.soccerbase.com

Here's a site _____

_____

3 www.handbag.com

This is a site _____

_____

4 www.carphonewarehouse.com

Here's a site _____

_____

5 www.tips4trips.com

Here's a site _____

_____

4 Relative clauses: who, which or neither

→ SB, Looking at grammar, p. 64

Match the sentence starters and the correct sentence elements to produce definitions. Leave out the relative pronoun where possible.

> 3 companies do / each other on / internet
> 1 writes pieces / computer software 1.
> 5 people can visit / give / get information / particular topic
> 7 organization calls in / look after / computer system
> 6 enjoy using / skills / break into secret (eg government) files / networks
> 8 organizations use / analyse / IT needs / problems / design general solutions / them
> 2 means 1,048,576 bytes / computer memory
> 4 people can use / send / same letter / many addresses

1 A computer programmer is someone _who_____

2 Mb is an abbreviation _which means_____

3 E-commerce is business _is_____

4 MailMerge is a program _that_____

5 A bulletin board is an internet site _which_____

6 Hackers are computer experts _who_____

7 Systems analysts are people _who_____

8 An IT technician is somebody _who_____

5 Why 'cellphones'?

→ SB, Technical reading, p. 67

Complete the labelling of the photos of a cellphone with words from the box.

antenna
battery
charger
contacts
display
display window
earpiece
keyboard
microphone
mouthpiece
speaker

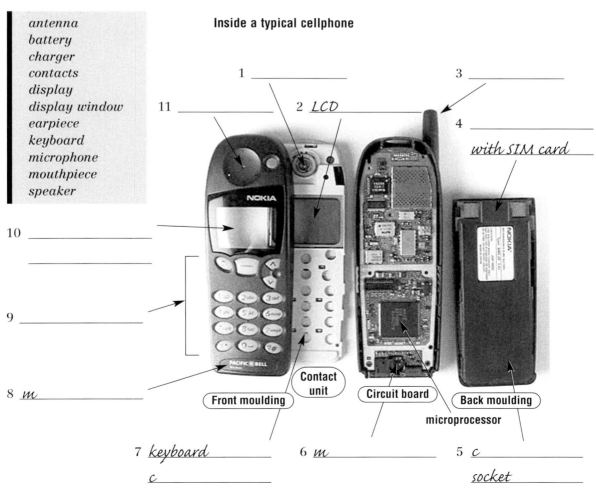

Inside a typical cellphone

1 _____   3 _____

11 _____   2 _LCD_   4 _____

with SIM card

10 _____
_____

9 _____

8 _m_____

Front moulding   Contact unit   Circuit board   Back moulding

microprocessor

7 _keyboard_   6 _m_____   5 _c_____

_c_____   _socket_____

5 Which road to the future?

1 Interpreting pie charts

→ SB, Text A, p. 69

A Study the pie chart again and complete the paragraph.

About one in 20 people goes to work _____

_____ [1], and roughly a tenth use a

_____ [2]. Approximately one in 25 relies

on _____ [3] ways of getting to work without a

car – for example, on foot or by bicycle. Altogether,

just over a fifth use these methods of travel to work.

By contrast, just under four out of five _____

_____ [4] to work.

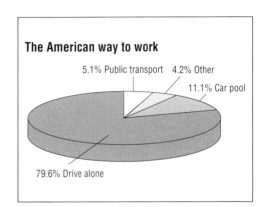

The American way to work

5.1% Public transport   4.2% Other
11.1% Car pool
79.6% Drive alone

B Now complete a similar paragraph about Henby Town Council's analysis of its rush-hour problems. Use forms from **2A** like these:

> about ▪ roughly ▪ approximately
> a quarter / a fifth / a tenth / two fifths / three quarters / ...
> *one in three / five / ten / ...
> *two / three / ... out of five / ten ...

(*Note: *one + in* ..., but with plurals, eg: *three + out of* ...)

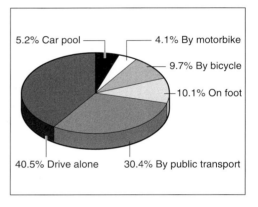

5.2% Car pool   4.1% By motorbike
9.7% By bicycle
10.1% On foot
40.5% Drive alone   30.4% By public transport

Only about a _____ [1] of the population avoids the use of motor transport completely

and travels into town by _____ [2] or on _____ [3]. As for people who at least

share motor transport with others, _____ [4] one _____ [5] uses a car

pool, and _____ [6] a further three _____ [7] go to work by public

_____ [8]. That leaves _____ [9] another one in 25 who travel in to work

_____ [10], along with a worrying two _____ [11] who continue to

drive alone to work by _____ [12].

2 Words: synonyms

→ SB, Text B, p. 72/3

A Find words in the text of similar meaning. (They are in the same order as in the text.)

1	cut	_____	2 as a result of _____
3	rising fast	_____	4 in the meantime _____
5	change over to	_____	6 prefer to _____
7	as well as	_____	8 worried _____
9	worldwide	_____	10 declining _____
11	in fact	_____	12 thinking about _____

B Rewrite this item from BBC News using words from **2A** to replace the underlined words.

Despite all the problems, it seems that most people in Britain would still <u>rather</u> _____ [1]
travel by car than <u>change over to</u> _____ [2] public transport, and this means that
road traffic figures are still <u>rising fast</u> _____ [3]. <u>In the meantime</u> _____ [4],
<u>worldwide</u> _____ [5] supplies of oil remain uncertain. Supplies from the Middle
East may <u>in fact</u> _____ [6] soon start <u>falling</u> _____ [7], and could be
<u>cut</u> _____ [8] severely <u>due to</u> _____ [9] more fighting in that part of
the world. According to Energy Minister Diane Shaw, the government has become increasingly
<u>concerned</u> _____ [10] and is now actively <u>thinking about</u> _____ [11]
a new, high-speed railway system as <u>well as</u> _____ [12] – for the first time –
charges for using the motorway system.

→ SB, Looking at
grammar, p. 74

3 The passive

A Put the following into the passive using the correct tenses. Leave out the by-agent when it
is unnecessary.

> **European transport on the ground**
> Across Europe, we are improving transport links. An Anglo-French company completed
> the Channel Tunnel in the 1990s. (But only after the massive costs had almost destroyed
> the company.) Again, the new Oresund Bridge has brought Danes and Swedes much closer.
> In Germany and France, new high-speed trains are reducing journey times. Then, when
> engineers finish the planned Messina Bridge, they will connect Sicily and mainland Italy.
> With this, they are going to give us the freedom to drive from the far north to the far south
> of our continent.

_____

_____

_____

_____

_____

_____

B Continue, putting the following into modal passive forms. No by-agents are needed.

> **European transport in the air**
> We need to improve air transport across Europe. Often, airport delays can cause major problems.
> And as a result, we will have to use much larger planes. In fact, we may build the first of these
> quite soon. We cannot do this, however, without major new airport development.
> First, though, we should deal with the chaos of European air traffic control. We must set up a
> single European system. With this, we could reduce overcrowding in European skies greatly.

_____

_____

_____

_____

4 The passive: mixed forms

Tony Bell has asked a mechanic to check a car he wants to buy. Complete the formal report using passive forms of the verbs in brackets.

Report for Mr Bell on Fiat Uno 1.0 litre, G105 NFW

The following points (note) _____ [1], and in my view the car (should +

not buy) _____ [2] in its present condition.

1) MOT*

Before anything else, the car (should + put) _____ [3] through its MOT.

All the problems (show) _____ [4] up by that.

2) Tyres

The two front tyres (need + change) _____ [5] . They (not

accept) _____ [6] if they (not change) _____ [7].

3) Bodywork

The front passenger door (badly/damage) _____ [8] in a crash,

and it (replace) _____ [9]. But it (not repaint) _____

_____ [10] yet, and that really (ought + do) _____ [11].

4) Exhaust

The box on the exhaust (have to + change) _____ [12]. The car

(certainly + fail) _____ [13] because of the hole in it.

---

* MOT = *TÜV*

5 Gears

→ SB, Technical reading, p. 77

Link the components on the left with their function on the right.

1 brakes		a enable the rider to pedal at a steady speed.
2 chain		b enable the rider to steer the bike.
3 frame		c enable the rider to turn the front sprocket-wheels.
4 gears		d enables the rider to sit on the bike.
5 handlebars		e guide the chain and provide it with traction.
6 mudguards		f protect the rider when travelling over rough ground.
7 pedals		g protect the rider from water, mud etc.
8 saddle		h provides fixings for all components.
9 shock-absorbers		i slow down and stop the bike.
10 sprocket-wheels		j transmits power to the rear sprocket-wheels.

1 ▢   2 ▢   3 ▢   4 ▢   5 ▢   6 ▢   7 ▢   8 ▢   9 ▢   10 ▢

6 Buying and selling

1 Vocabulary: retail outlets

→ SB, Focus, p. 78

Which kinds of retail outlet(s) probably suit these people best?

1 JANE   I just don't have the time to go to the shops. Obviously, I find other ways of shopping much better.

Jane probably prefers shopping _____ , from a _____ _____ _____ or from an agent ____ _____ .

2 GESA   I love shopping – it gets me out of the house and I meet people.

Gesa probably likes going to the _____ , to _____ _____ or to an outdoor _____ , of course.

3 BEN   I don't like shopping much, but I do like to look at things properly and get advice, if necessary. I prefer places with everything under one roof.

Ben probably often does his shopping at a _____ _____ or hypermarket.

4 ALAN   It's great. Now they've solved the security problem; click-click and away you go.

Alan definitely does a lot of his shopping on the _____ .

5 ANN   You'll see me there on Wednesdays and Saturdays – you meet people, the food is fresh, and you're helping small producers.

Ann definitely goes to the _____ on these days.

6 JOHN   Perhaps I'm conservative. I'm happy to pay a little more for personal service and proper advice from a real human-being.

John certainly likes to do his shopping at _____ _____ , the _____ or perhaps from an agent _____ _____ .

2 Vocabulary: synonyms

→ SB, Text A, p. 79

Replace the underlined word/expression in the sentences with a word from the introduction and the text as far as line 30 **without** making any other changes.

1 I think we need the help of a retailing adviser *consultant* with this problem.

2 I buy lots of books and CDs on the internet _____ .

3 When does the meeting begin _____ ?

4 Ann has always had her doubts _____ about IT.

5 Some sellers _____ just changed 'DM' to '€' on 1 January 2002.

6 A lot of people very much like _____ getting out of the house.

7 I don't think this is the difficulty _____ that people say it is.

8 Don't interrupt _____ until I have finished my sentence.

9 Debit card payments are much more secure _____ now.

10 You were crazy to buy that mobile without knowing the precise _____ price.

3 Vocabulary: spending

→ SB, Text B, p. 81

Complete the text with information from the pie chart.

Computer, mobile (personal communication)

Hi-fi, CDs, DVDs (personal entertainment)

"Incidentals", incl. school

Personal transport eg car, scooter

€12 €5

€13

€37

€15

€18

Personal appearance eg clothes, fashion

Socialising incl. food, drink, cinema, disco etc

Average expenditure of German 18-year-olds (€100)

You are an average _____ ¹ 18-year old with _____ ² in your pocket. What will you spend this money on? Well, according to statistics on _____ ³, you will spend well over a third of it, €37, on _____ ⁴, a _____ ⁵ or a scooter, for example. You enjoy going out with your friends, so you will spend the next biggest amount, _____ ⁶, on socialising. This includes expenditure on food and _____ ⁷, as well as such activities as going to the _____ ⁸ or disco. Of course, people who enjoy going out also like to look good, so it's no surprise that you will spend quite a lot of money, _____ ⁹ in every €100, on clothes and _____ ¹⁰. Well, now you have just _____ ¹¹ left. What will you buy with them? €13 will go on personal _____ ¹² and _____ ¹³ on communication, eg your mobile. That leaves you with just _____ ¹⁴ to spend on everything else, including _____ ¹⁵.

4 Vocabulary: compound nouns

→ SB, Text B, p. 81

A   Form 2-word compound nouns by adding a noun from the texts to the nouns in the list.

1 dress   *code*

2 fashion   _____

3 school   _____

4 crime   _____

5 street   _____

6 mobile   _____

7 PIN   _____

8 industry   _____

9 life   _____

10 service   _____

B   Complete the sentences with suitable compounds. Be careful about plural forms.

1 Many schools have a _____ that says what pupils may not wear.

2 The alternative is to have a _____ where all pupils have to wear the same things.

3 Mugging is an example of the kind of _____ that is causing a big increase in UK _____ .

4 In America, _____ are called 'cellphones'.

5 The English word for 'Dienstleister' is _____ .

6 Young children learn very basic _____ such as how to get on with other people at kindergarten.

5   If-sentences, Types I and II

Put the verbs into the correct tenses for the type of if-sentence shown. Look at the example first.

1 II If the shop (have) _had_ videocameras, there (not be) _would not be_ so much

    shoplifting.

2 I I (not wear) _____ a school uniform even if the school (say) _____ I must.

3 I If you (come) _____ to school in a combat jacket again, you (be) _____

    sent home.

4 II People (still + steal) _____ mobile phones even if they (be)

    _____ protected by PIN codes.

5 I Ian says that if we (make) _____ PIN codes compulsory, violent crime (probably

    + increase) _____ .

6 II If schools (teach) _____ more life skills, the under-25s (be) _____

    more independent.

7 II Young people (not steal) _____ mobile phones if the rest of us

    (not see) _____ them as status symbols.

8 I If all the small shopkeepers in the town centre (close) _____ , where (old

    people/do) _____ their shopping?

9 II If consumers (pay) _____ for better service, small specialist shops (not have to)

    _____ close.

10 II Jim says that if internet retailers (be) _____ properly managed, they (do)

    _____ much better.

11 II Hilary feels that if her school (introduce) _____ school uniforns, it (not

    agree) _____ with democratic ideas.

6   Too much of a good thing?

Complete the sentences with the missing prepositions or particles.

| about |
| by |
| for |
| from |
| in (2x) |
| of (6x) |
| on |
| out |
| over |
| to (3x) |
| up to |
| with |
| within |

According _to_ [1] an EU directive _of_ [2] 23 October 2001, workers may only use vibrating machines _____ [3] a maximum _____ [4] two _____ [5] four hours, depending _____ [6] the level _____ [7] vibration. This directive is fine _____ [8] the point _____ [9] view _____ [10] workers' health because the body should not be exposed _____ [11] too much vibration. Although the new directive could cost British companies _____ [12] €36.3 billion _____ [13] a period _____ [14] ten years, it has been welcomed _____ [15] health experts _____ [16] the UK. Experts point _____ [17] that companies equipped _____ [18] modern machines _____ [19] modern buildings have nothing to worry _____ [20] because they are already well _____ [21] the new vibration limits.

1 Crossword: wordfield – the business world

→ SB, Focus, p. 87;
Text A, p. 88

Complete the crossword. (The words are not always the same grammatical form as in the texts.)

Across

1 People usually get … mainly to make money.
2 He always … his staff on the last Thursday of the month.
3 Here at this factory we … CD cases.
4 We give new production … a week's training before they start.
5 From my new … I can look out across the city.
6 Closing the factory will have a bad … on the town's economy.
7 Volkswagen is a … organization with operations in many different countries.
8 The company … the old factory and bought a big, new one instead.
9 The … of the old factory was completed quickly and then we moved out.
10 Companies in Mexico often pay only the … wage, which is very low.
11 The same companies are also often big polluters and cause a lot of … problems.

Down

1 Teresa was so lazy that the company finally gave her the … .
2 Millions of Chinese are very … and hardly make enough money to live.
3 The company makes a very good … of 25% on everything it sells.
4 These days, every factory has to be very careful about the health and … of people working there.
5 Thanks to … , Europe has lost many older industries to low-cost Asia.
6 We … 50 staff at Head Office and 2,400 in our three factories.
7 Peter's team have … an exciting new bicycle, and we want to start production as soon as possible.
8 We have to start making money soon or we'll go out of … .
9 In his new job, Tim … more money but the work was much harder.
10 This isn't Japanese. Look at the label. It says '… in China'.
11 Ten people have … their jobs because the company has too few orders.

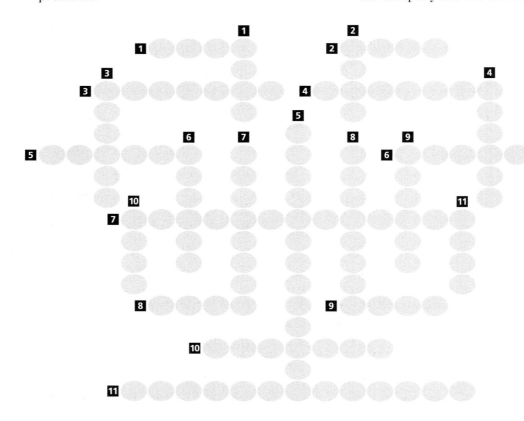

2 The past perfect

→ SB, Looking at grammar, p. 92

Put all the verbs in brackets into the past perfect where appropriate, or else just the simple past. Sometimes you will need the passive.

Jackie (check) _____ [1] the calendar. Today (be) _____ [2] exactly three months since the day she (finish) _____ [3] her college course in business studies, and she still (not find) _____ 4 a job. She (feel) _____ [5] a little desperate as the others – Mum, Dad and brother Charlie – (leave) _____ [6] the house to go to work.

Then the post (arrive) _____ [7] and Jackie quickly (pick up) _____ [8] the two letters for her, both official-looking. The first letter (be) _____ [9] very short, and she (read) _____ [10] it quickly. She (reject) _____ [11]. The second (be) _____ [12] from Fast-track Data Systems, where she (go) _____ [13] for an interview just the week before. Thinking back now, she (feel) _____ [14] that she (do) _____ [15] well. She also (remember) _____ [16] that she (really like) _____ [17] the people and the company. Nervously, she (open) _____ [18] the letter and her eyes (move) _____ [19] down the page. ... 'WOW!' she suddenly (shout) _____ [20]. 'I've got a job!'

3 If-sentences type III

→ SB, Looking at grammar, p. 92

Form *if*-sentences type III. (The *if* part may be in first or second position.)

1 the factory (stay) in business / Ted Best and his friends (continue) to work there

_____

_____

2 (not see) the success of his cousin's window-cleaning business / (look for) another factory job like his friends

_____

_____

3 and (not consider) starting a courier business / his cousin (not give) him his old van

_____

_____

4 (not start) just at that time / (miss) the chance of a new city council courier contract

_____

_____

5 (not get) that contract / it (be) much harder to build up his business

_____

6 Soon, the job (become) too much / he (not invite) his old friend Rick Eastwood to join him

_____

_____

That was the start ... And this is where he is today – with all his old friends from the factory.

4 Words: adverbs and prepositions

Add the missing prepositions and adverbs. Choose from the following.

> *for* ▪ *from* ▪ *in* ▪ *into* ▪ *near* ▪ *of* ▪ *on* ▪ *over* ▪ *to* ▪ *with*

My name is Florian Ambroziak and I'm _____ [1] a small town quite _____ [2] Warsaw _____ [3] Poland. I used to work _____ [4] an engineering company supplying equipment _____ [5] farms all _____ [6] our area. But most _____ [7] the farmers were _____ [8] financial trouble, and a lot couldn't pay _____ [9] what they had bought. Because _____ [10] that my employer went bankrupt. Luckily for us, Auto-Dubois were looking _____ [11] a cheaper place to produce than the UK, and they decided _____ [12] our area. They actually took _____ [13] my old employer's factory. They also employed a lot of the old staff – people _____ [14] engineering skills like myself. _____ [15] course, Auto-Dubois lost several months _____ [16] production, and they had to put a lot _____ [17] money _____ [18] the move _____ [19] England _____ [20] Poland and _____ [21] training staff, but they seem very happy _____ [22] what's happened.

5 Tracking see-through people

→ SB, Technical reading, p. 95

Join the sentence halves to make true statements.

1 All human fingerprints have a

2 All humans have unique biometric traits

3 As a means of identification, fingerprinting

4 Before the coming of computerised image scanning,

5 Biometric traits include fingerprints and palmprints

6 In future, fingerprinting will probably continue

7 It was estimated in 2001 that

8 People are willing to accept finger printing

9 Some firms have developed portable fingerprint

10 Thanks to the new scanning technology,

a as well as body odour and the pattern of the iris.

b because they are familiar with it from crime films.

c fingerprinting has become fast and reliable.

d reading fingerprints was difficult and tiring.

e scanners that are smaller than a pack of cards.

f that make them different from everybody else.

g there were 6.1 billion people on earth.

h to be the most common biometric technology.

i unique pattern of arches, loops and whorls.

j was first adopted by London's police in 1901.

1   2   3   4   5   6   7   8   9   10

1 Vocabulary: recycling

→ SB, Focus, p. 96

You live in Germany. Complete the table with material from the box.

Types of waste
bio-degradable
non-degradable, non-recyclable
recyclable
special

Methods of disposal
black/dark grey waste bin
brown/green compost bin
glass recycling container
paper recycling container
return to store
toxic waste collection point
yellow 'Grüner Punkt' bin/sack

Waste	Type	Method of disposal
1 a broken cup	*non-degradable, non-recyclable*	*black/dark grey waste bin*
2 an old computer		
3 beer crate		
4 damaged CD		
5 drinks can		
6 empty jars		
7 food leftovers		
8 old cardboard boxes		
9 old engine oil		
10 old exercise books		
11 old rubber boots		
12 old socks		
13 plastic packaging		
14 used teabags		

2 Vocabulary: noun forms

→ SB, Text A, p. 97

Find a noun form of these verbs in the text. They are in the same order.

1 (to) industrialise *industry*

2 (to) waste

3 (to) confer

4 (to) lobby

5 (to) dispose

6 (to) govern

7 (to) equip

8 (to) cook

9 (to) refrigerate

10 (to) live

11 (to) compute

12 (to) generate

3 Water in Benidorm

→ SB, Text B, p. 99

Look at the text and cross out the wrong number in the sentences to make true statements.

1 About *48,000*/50,000 people live permanently in Benidorm.
2 At the moment, the population rises to about *320,000/330,000* in the summer.
3 The report says that Benidorm has *131/132* hotels at present, but *4/5* more are in the process of being built.
4 When the building is finished, Benidorm will have a summer population of around *545,000/550,000*.
5 It is amazing that a medium-sized town like Benidorm has *30,000/30,200* swimming-pools.
6 Wells which were once *15/16* metres deep and now *five/six* times that depth.
7 Between *1960/1970* and *1990/2000*, tourist arrivals grew to *650/670* million a year, an increase of *nine/ten* times the figure for *1950/1960*.
8 It is estimated that tourist arrivals will continue to grow by *25/30* million a year worldwide.

4 Indirect speech

→ SB, Looking at grammar, p. 100/101

You are a journalist. You are attending a press conference for foreign travel journalists in Madrid. Put the statements, questions and requests into indirect speech for your report. Use the introductory verbs in brackets.

Statements

1 The minister: I hope you will listen to the experts. (begin by saying)

– The minister _____ that _____ the journalists

_____ to the experts.

2 Engineer: It is true that we will have to drill much deeper for water, but I do not think that this is a problem. (say, add)

– An _____ that it _____ true that they _____

_____ much deeper for water, but _____ that _____

_____ a problem.

3 Hotel-owner: Farmers are good at complaining, but they are not so good at conserving the water they already have. (feel)

– A _____ that farmers _____ good at complaining, but they

_____ so good at conserving the water they already _____ .

4 Tourist manager: I'm sure that 30,000 swimming-pools sounds crazy, but most of them are only filled once in their service lives. (agree, emphasise)

– A tourist manager _____ that 30,000 swimming-pools _____ crazy, but

_____ that most of them _____ once in their service lives.

Questions

5 Jim Snow: Minister, do you agree that water shortages will make further growth impossible? (want to know)

– Jim Snow _____

that water shortages _____ further growth impossible.

6 Lisa Bach: Mr Cordes, what do you think can be done to help farmers? (ask)

– Lisa Bach _____ Mr Cordes _____ be done

to help farmers.

7   Jean Duval: Mrs Gonzales, how much did Spain invest in tourism last year? (want to know)

– Jean Duval _____ from Mrs Gonzales _____

_____ in tourism _____ .

8   Lisa Bach: Mr Cordes, do you think it right that Benidorm uses so much water when animals are dying of thirst? (ask)

– Lisa Bach _____ it right that Benidorm

_____ so much water when animals _____ of thirst.

Requests

9   Please read our press statement before the conference. (an official/ask/us)

– _____ press statement

before the conference.

10 Please say the name of the person who you want to answer your question. (the chairwoman/tell/Lisa Bach)

– _____ the name of

the person who _____ to answer _____ question.

11 Please speak English or some people won't understand you. (the chairwoman/ask/Julia Asvar)

– _____ English or

some people _____ .

12 Don't smoke during the press conference, please. (a security guard/tell/Jean Duval)

– _____

during the press conference.

5 How a horizontal axis wind turbine works

→ SB, Technical reading, p. 104

Find a technical word or expression in the box for the general words or expressions in the list.

Box		List	Answer
connected to		1 change (rpm)	*translate*
cut out		2 dynamo	_____
cylindrical		3 joined to	_____
direct-drive		4 machine housing	_____
generator		5 plastic	_____
nacelle		6 propeller	_____
polyester		7 round	_____
resilient		8 spins (per minute)	_____
resist		9 stand up to	_____
revolutions		10 stop	_____
rotate around		11 tough and flexible	_____
rotor		12 turning (mechanism)	_____
~~translate~~		13 turn round	_____
yaw		14 without a gearbox	_____

Unit 9 Zero tolerance?

1 Wordfield: crimes

→ SB, Focus, p. 105

A Find 15 types of crime in the word square (*senkrecht oder waagerecht*).

r	o	b	b	e	r	y	c	d	r	u	n	k	d	r	i	v	i	n	g
m	v	u	c	x	a	p	l	o	i	t	z	v	e	r	x	w	q	l	m
t	g	r	s	x	p	b	s	h	o	p	l	i	f	t	i	n	g	b	s
h	f	g	v	b	e	o	h	j	l	b	r	x	o	i	w	q	m	v	m
e	r	L	w	o	n	m	a	n	s	l	a	u	g	h	t	e	r	b	u
f	c	a	v	s	k	j	n	r	z	t	s	h	c	i	l	g	n	b	g
t	v	r	q	m	u	r	d	e	r	j	s	k	b	j	v	f	p	o	g
o	p	y	l	f	c	r	e	w	l	p	a	d	x	a	b	r	k	x	l
w	s	x	j	n	h	g	v	i	u	t	u	m	v	c	y	a	t	r	i
k	i	d	n	a	p	p	i	n	g	v	l	s	d	k	t	u	m	l	n
t	r	f	b	n	i	u	m	v	r	e	t	j	h	i	b	d	v	c	g
c	v	a	n	d	a	l	i	s	m	j	k	t	r	n	d	q	w	p	o
e	r	g	t	w	m	j	u	n	b	g	f	m	u	g	g	i	n	g	k

B Complete the following using words from **1A** or other grammatical forms of these words.

1 Jason Bell was stopped by a store detective for _____ as he tried to leave with two shirts under his jacket.

2 A _____ broke into Mrs Hislop's flat the other night.

3 A total of 19 terrorists _____ four different planes in America on September 11th, 2001.

4 Two men with guns came into the post office and _____ it of €5,000.

5 The three _____ sent the parents a note instructing them to pay €1,000,000 for their daughter's safe return.

6 After the crash, the test showed that Alan Barnes had drunk twice as much as the legal limit, and he lost his licence for _____ .

7 The court decided that Rachel West had had to kill the man to save her own life, and she was therefore found guilty of _____ and not of _____ .

2 Wordfield: language of change

Continue the description of each chart using the language given.

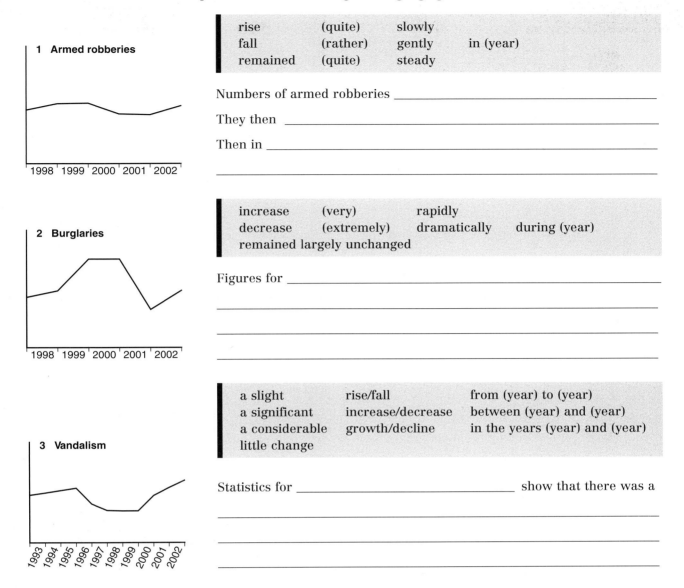

1 Armed robberies

rise	(quite)	slowly	
fall	(rather)	gently	in (year)
remained	(quite)	steady	

Numbers of armed robberies _____

They then _____

Then in _____

_____

2 Burglaries

increase	(very)	rapidly	
decrease	(extremely)	dramatically	during (year)
remained largely unchanged			

Figures for _____

_____

_____

_____

3 Vandalism

a slight	rise/fall	from (year) to (year)
a significant	increase/decrease	between (year) and (year)
a considerable	growth/decline	in the years (year) and (year)
little change		

Statistics for _____ show that there was a

_____

_____

_____

3 Words: connectors

Cross out the incorrect connectors to complete the paragraph.

Because/Although[1] the idea of youth courts may seem strange, they are becoming popular across the USA. *So far/Moreover*[2], there are nearly 900 such courts in 46 states, *and/for*[3] the numbers are continuing to grow. Many of these courts are operated by cities *but/and*[4] youth service programmes. *Moreover/Though*[5], many schools – *as/since*[6] one might expect – have started to try using them. *Despite/Instead of*[7] a visit to the school principal's office, students may now find themselves in front of a court of other pupils. Offenders may appear for something less serious *such as/in other words*[8] smoking or for something worse – theft, *by contrast/for instance*[9]. The offender first has to answer all the questions of the jury (*die Geschworenen*) of students *and/or*[10] then accept their punishment. The idea is *that since/in the first place*[11] peer pressure has often led the offender to do something wrong, peer pressure (*Gruppenzwang*) may *nevertheless/also*[12] help to stop the offender from doing wrong again.

4 Verb + infinitive; verb + ~ing

→ SB, Looking at grammar, p. 109

Complete the following, using pairs of verbs from the list

> *avoid/think about* ▪ *fail/notice* ▪ *keep/find* ▪ *learn/be* ▪ *prevent things from/get* ▪
> *remember/keep* ▪ *seem/say* ▪ *start/include* ▪ *succeed in/develop* ▪ *stop/push* ▪
> *suggest/report* ▪ *try/do*

After a number of killings in schools across America, Dr Peter Berry, an expert on youth and violence, has this to say about the problem.

When a school killing happens, I know it _____ [1] to us that our

world has gone mad. However, we must _____ [2] it in perspective:

these killings are very rare. The trouble is that people around a potential killer often

_____ [3] various signals and _____ [4]

it when somebody is acting strangely.

What we must all _____ [5] first of all is to reduce bullying *(tyrannisieren)* and

_____ [6] kinder and more friendly towards other students – all of them, including

the 'outsiders'. We must _____ [7] them away and _____ [8]

them more. I say this because we _____ [9] that these killers are also young people

who have not _____ [10] strong relationships *(Beziehung)*

with other people. The second thing I would say is this. If you see somebody really acting or

speaking strangely, then it is important to _____ [11] out

of control. If this happened, I would strongly _____ [12] what

you have noticed to a teacher or to some other adult at school.

5 Is shoplifting really a crime?

→ SB, Technical reading, p. 112

Match the drawings to the methods of fighting shoplifting below.

a fixing electronic tags to articles
b hiring security guards
c joining articles together with wire
d locking goods away in a display cabinet
e putting articles out of reach
f rewarding customers for catching shoplifters
g using CCTV cameras to watch customers

1 Quotas

→ SB, Text A, p. 114

Cross out the wrong connectors to make true statements.

1 John Carr was not chosen *although*/~~*as*/*but*~~ he was as well qualified as Grant Summers.
2 John says that Grant was chosen simply *and*/*because*/*for* he is black.
3 The party has a quota system *although*/*however*/*so* members of minorities have a big advantage.
4 John says the quota system means some people have no chance, *but*/*however*/*yet* good they are.
5 John went to court *but*/*if*/*when* his lawyers told him he would probably win.
6 The basic question is *however*/*nonetheless*/*whether* the quota system is really 'automatic selection'.
7 The European court said 'automatic selection' was illegal, *and*/*but*/*yet* it said nothing about quotas as such.
8 Quotas are used in Germany, *and*/*though*/*where* there are many more woman politicians than in Britain.
9 Helen Budd thinks that if the two men are really equal, *for*/*then*/*yet* random selection is the only fair way to choose between them.
10 Mike Davis writes that members of minorities *and*/*still*/*yet* have to compete with members of their own or other minorities.

2 Australian aborigines

→ SB, Text B, p. 116

A Complete the sentences with the missing prepositions.

1 Qantas used a photo _____ Carol Napangardi _____ an ad that called her 'the spirit _____ Australia'.

2 Although Carol was glad _____ the money _____ the time, she is now living _____ a shack _____ the deserts _____ Western Australia.

3 The Aborigines are popular _____ advertisers _____ selling Australia _____ foreigners, but they are never used _____ advertising products _____ home.

4 The sad fact is that the Aborigines live _____ the edge _____ Australian society and play little part _____ the life _____ their own country.

5 Although Aboriginal art _____ didgeridoo music _____ dot paintings is used _____ car companies, _____ example, to sell their products, these companies seldom give a job _____ a real Aborigine.

6 The souvenirs sold _____ tourists _____ tens _____ millions _____ dollars a year were probably imported _____ Asia or even made _____ European backpackers to pay _____ their holiday.

B Read the speech bubbles and say who is speaking.

1 a car salesman

2 a copy writer   *a*

3 a journalist

4 a Qantas spokesman

5 a Queensland trader

6 Carol Napangardi

7 Cathy Freeman

8 Sol Bellear

> Foreigners are fascinated by the Aborigines, so of course we use them. Unfortunately, this doesn't apply to Australians. **a**

> I don't understand the argument. Do companies whose ads use Mozart have to employ Austrians, or what? **b**

> I was really shocked by some of the statistics I found when I was researching this story. **d**

> It sounds a lot of money, I know, but we're a big family. Do you think we like living here? **c**

> Look, I have to get this stuff from Taiwan because the Aborigines want too much for the real thing, OK? **e**

> This is all show. Look at how most Aborigines live. It's about as romantic as hell. **f**

> We'd like to employ more Aborigines, but they just don't apply for the jobs. **g**

> Well, of course they said I wasn't given this great honour just because I'm an Aborigine, but I'm not so sure, I'm afraid. **h**

3 Participle structures

→ SB, Looking at grammar, p. 117

A Shorten the sentences by replacing the underlined parts with present or past participles. Look at the example first.

1 <u>When he landed</u> in Australia, James Cook first ordered three sailors to find fresh water.

On landing in Australia, James Cook first ordered three sailors to find fresh water.

2 <u>Because he thought that Australia</u> was uninhabited, he claimed it for Britain.

_____ was uninhabited, he claimed it for Britain.

3 <u>While they were searching</u> for a river, the three men met a group of Aborigines.

_____ for a river, the three men met a group of Aborigines.

4 <u>Because they were frightened</u> of these stange men, at first the Aborigines ran away.

_____ of these stange men, at first the Aborigines ran away.

5 <u>When he was told</u> about the Aborigines, Cook was very surprised.

_____ about the Aborigines, Cook was very surprised.

6 Cook told his men to build a fort <u>because he did not know</u> if the Aborigines were friendly.

_____ if the Aborigines were friendly, Cook told his men to build a fort.

7 <u>While they were cutting down</u> trees for the fort, the men saw a larger group of Aborigines.

_____ trees for the fort, the men saw a larger group of Aborigines.

8 Cook's men picked up their guns <u>as they saw</u> the Aborigines were carrying spears.

_____ the Aborigines were carrying spears, Cook's men picked up their guns.

B Shorten the relative clauses with present or past participles. Look at the example first.

1 "Quotas that are used to help minorities are illegal," says John Carr.

"Quotas _used_ to help minorities are illegal," says John Carr.

2 Countries like Sweden that use quotas have many more women in top jobs.

_____ have many more women in top jobs.

3 The court case that is being brought by John Carr could lead to a change in the law.

_____ could lead to a change in the law.

4 Lawyers who specialise in European law say that John has a good chance of winning.

_____ say that John has a

good chance of winning.

5 The black man who was chosen by the selection committee was the better candidate anyhow.

_____ was the better

candidate anyhow.

6 Positive discrimination that gives some people an unfair advantage is already illegal.

_____ an unfair advantage

is already illegal.

7 The British-Indian woman who was recently promoted to chief inspector was on TV last night.

_____

was on TV last night.

8 The European court that ruled against automatic selection said nothing about quotas.

_____

said nothing about quotas.

---

4 High-tech is not the only tech

→ SB, Technical reading, p. 120

Complete the photo description with words and expression from the box.

are walking
at top left
background
barrels
clearly
easy
garden roller
girls
hidden
left to right
next
skirt
to the left
to the right
water

In the photo _____ [1], we see four African _____ [2].
A fifth girl is just out of the picture _____ [3]. All the girls
are pushing Hippo Rollers®, which are plastic _____ [4]
that can be filled with _____ [5] and then pushed along
like a _____ [6]. Moving from _____ [7],
the first girl's barrel is out of the picture _____ [8].
We can see the _____ [9] two girls' barrels, one green and
one blue, _____ [10]. The relaxed way in which the girls
_____ [11] shows that the barrels are _____ [12] to
push along. The fourth girl in the _____ [13] is
evidently (*offensichtlich*) pushing a barrel, too, though it is
_____ [14] behind the girl wearing a light blue _____ [15].

1 Words: compound nouns

→ SB, Text A, p. 122;
Text B, p. 124

Add partners from the box to the key words.

> *blueprint* ▪ *champion* ▪ *crops* ▪ *economy* ▪ *engineering* ▪ *nature* ▪ *race* ▪ *rights* ▪
> *soya* ▪ *supply* ▪ *trade*

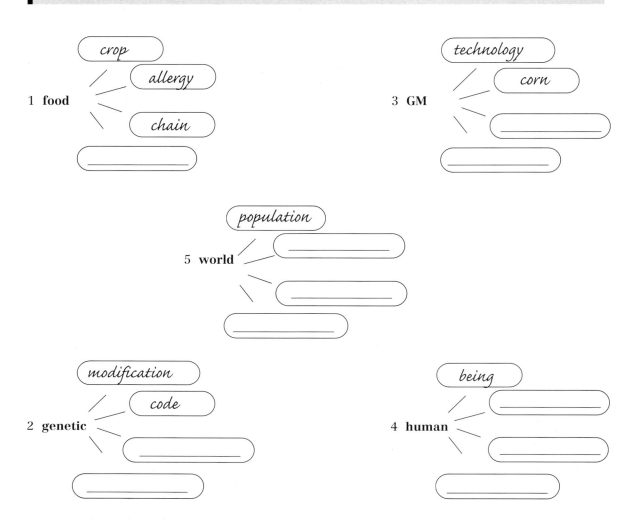

1 **food** — *crop* / *allergy* / *chain* / _____

3 **GM** — *technology* / *corn* / _____

5 **world** — *population* / _____ / _____

2 **genetic** — *modification* / *code* / _____

4 **human** — *being* / _____ / _____

2 Words: synonyms

→ SB, Text B, p. 124

A Find words in the texts that mean the same as the following. (The words are in the same order.)

Text 1: Harry's son makes history

1 alterations _____

2 revealed _____

3 was made up of _____

4 faulty _____

5 concerned _____

6 illnesses _____

Text 2: DNA lesson

1 managing _____

2 government _____

3 do-able _____

4 holds within it _____

5 natural ability _____

6 showing _____

Text 3: Playing with nature's plan		Text 4: The damage done	
1 design	_____	1 sounded loudly	_____
2 created	_____	2 very quiet	_____
3 inserted	_____	3 start	_____
4 unsafe	_____	4 very unusual	_____
5 thoroughly	_____	5 falling to pieces	_____
6 in the direction of	_____	6 resulted from	_____

B Use words from **2A** to rewrite the following, changing words that are underlined.

Recent research has <u>revealed</u> _____ ¹ that the human genetic code <u>is made up of</u> _____ ² about 40,000 genes and that these contain the complete genetic <u>design</u> _____ ³ for each human life. Research also <u>shows</u> _____ ⁴ that our various sorts of intelligence and <u>natural ability</u> _____ ⁵ are <u>created</u> _____ ⁶ by numbers of genes acting together in ways we do not understand. Most scientists are therefore <u>concerned</u> _____ ⁷ that it would be both very difficult and very <u>unsafe</u> _____ ⁸ to try to have extra genes <u>inserted</u> _____ ⁹ to give a child these qualities. We are living through the <u>start</u> _____ ¹⁰ of a new era in medical history in which scientists are learning to make <u>alterations</u> _____ ¹¹ to our genes and are finding out how to cure some of the <u>very unusual</u> _____ ¹² <u>illnesses</u> _____ ¹³ that <u>result from</u> _____ ¹⁴ a <u>faulty</u> _____ ¹⁵ genetic make-up.

3 Tenses

→ SB, Looking at grammar, p. 125

Complete the text using the right form of the verbs in brackets. You have to use either the simple present, present continuous, simple past, present perfect or the passive.

The global population (grow) _____ ¹ rapidly, but unfortunately the world's supply of food (not increase) _____ ² at the same rate. In many parts of the world pests and diseases (destroy) _____ ³ crops as they grow and every year we also (lose) _____ ⁴ farmland to deserts, roads and buildings. Starvation (be) _____ ⁵ now a major world-wide problem. In the last few years scientists (use) _____ ⁶ GM technology to produce better crops with better yields. For example, they (develop) _____ ⁷ new crops that can grow in deserts and on salty land. A few years ago scientists also (create) _____ ⁸ a new kind of rice. They (add) _____ ⁹ genes from peas that contain vitamin A. (Estimate) _____ ¹⁰ that this rice could save two million children every year that suffer from vitamin A deficiency.

4 If-sentences types I, II and III

→ SB, Looking at grammar, p. 125

Expand the sentence elements to make correct if-sentences.

1 I / (be) / David Peters' position / don't think / (want) / sue / parents

_____

_____

2 on the other hand / I think / (have) / test like Harry / Sophie West / technology (be) available

_____

_____

3 / (be) very difficult / feed / world / global population (reach) eleven billion

_____

_____

4 big biotech companies argue that / farmers (grow) / GM crops / they (quickly produce) bigger / better crops / ever before

_____

_____

5 / laboratory near Marseilles / (be) more careful / mutant 'superweed' (not escape) / Mediterranean / few years ago.

_____

_____

6 even / that (not happen) / there (be) environmental damage from other causes / same period of time

_____

_____

5 DNA – Nature's operating system

→ SB, Technical reading, p. 128

Say if the following statements are true (T), false (F) or you cannot say because the information is not in the text (?).

	T	F	?
1 Europeans very much for GM techniques for medical purposes.			
2 Americans are less worried about GM than Europeans are.			
3 Most Europeans are against using GM techniques to change food.			
4 Scientists are frustrated by public criticism of GM research.			
5 The writer uses chickens are an example of natural selection.			
6 DNA is the 'operating system' of only the human body.			
7 In the past, genetic modification was carried out by natural selection.			
8 Wheat is often seen as a 'natural food', but it is really 'GM grass'.			
9 Critics are worried that GM plants could destroy natural ones.			
10 Diabetics could be helped by a GM plant that produces cheap human insulin.			

12 Europe

1 The European economy

→ SB, Text A, p. 130

A Which products are countries particularly famous for? Link the countries on the left to the products on the right.

Britain

Denmark

Finland

France

Germany

Italy

Ireland

Netherlands

Spain

Sweden

cars

dairy produce

package holidays

pharmaceuticals

mobile phones

computer hardware

household equipment

packaging

flowers

wine

B All the statements below are factually wrong. Correct them by crossing out the mistake and giving the correct information on the right.

1 The Wall Street crash happened in ~~2015~~. _2011_

2 London is now the world's biggest financial centre.

3 Growth in the euro zone has been high for the last four years.

4 The EU is importing workers from Asia, Eastern Europe and Australia.

5 The population of the EU has grown to over 470 million people.

6 From north to south, the EU stretches from Finland to Greece.

7 David Owen analysed productivity in Europe.

8 In the USA, Detroit is the centre of aircraft production.

9 Mr Owen thinks Spain makes the best wine in Europe.

10 Mr Owen thinks life could become tough for carmakers in Oxford.

◼ 2 English in Europe

A Link a sentence part from list A to one from list B to make true statements.

A	B
1 A survey of EU citizens found that	a as 'linguistic nationalists' like to claim.
2 A large majority of Europeans thinks that	b as long as they don't have to use it.
3 About 16% of the EU's citizens speak	c can only speak their own language.
4 Over 40% of respondents said that	d English as a native language.
5 Anti-English feeling is not as common	e English is becoming Europe's *lingua franca*.
6 Having English will help workers to	f everybody should learn English.
7 Even now, nearly half of all EU citizens	g get jobs all over the single market.
8 Some people say they have a second language	h they could speak English.

1 _____ 2 _____ 3 _____ 4 _____ 5 _____ 6 _____ 7 _____ 8 _____

B Describe the column graph by completing the text with the missing information.

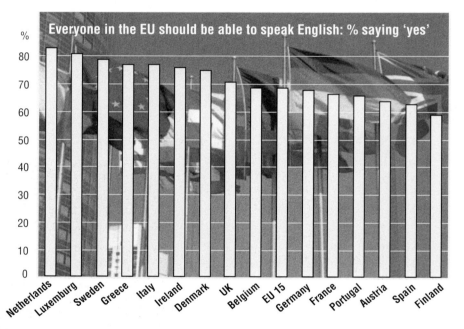

Everyone in the EU should be able to speak English: % saying 'yes'

Countries (horizontal axis): Netherlands, Luxemburg, Sweden, Greece, Italy, Ireland, Denmark, UK, Belgium, EU 15, Germany, France, Portugal, Austria, Spain, Finland

The *graph* ¹ shows the percentage of respondents from the different EU _____ ² who answered "_____ ³" to the question "Do you think everyone in the _____ ⁴ should be able to speak _____ ⁵?". The horizontal axis shows the _____ ⁶ countries and the average result for the _____ ⁷ as a whole; the vertical _____ ⁸ shows a scale from 0 to _____ % ⁹. With over 80% saying "Yes", the _____ ¹⁰ is most in agreement with the idea, closely followed by _____ ¹¹ with 80%. At the other end of the scale, less than _____ % ¹² of respondents in _____ ¹³ think everyone should learn English, but that is the only country to fall below the 60% mark. Of the "Big _____ ¹⁴ " with populations of over 55 million people, Italy scores highest, followed by the UK, _____ ¹⁵ and France. However, with only _____ ¹⁶ exceptions, all countries are in a narrow band of less than 20 percentage points, which explains the high EU _____ ¹⁷ score of just over 68%.

3 Problem plurals

→ SB, Looking at grammar, p. 133

Cross out the incorrect form.

1 *Tatort ~~are~~/is* a popular German TV *serie/series.*
2 Do you realise what they do to *geese/gooses* to make liver paté?
3 Ben lost three *teeth/teeths* in the accident.
4 I need a smaller *pliers/pair of pliers* for this job.
5 Not *much/many* British cattle *has/have* BSE now.
6 Please call the firm and ask when the goods *are/is* arriving, OK?
7 That shop sells exotic food like tropical *fish/fishes.*
8 The Japanese *are/is* by far the richest *people/peoples* in Asia.
9 The police *are/is* questioning two *mans/men* about the fire.
10 Another big steel works *was/were* closed last week.
11 There *are/is* so many *deer/deers* in Europe now that they are damaging the forests.
12 This *binocular/pair of binoculars was/were* made in Jena.
13 Tomatoes are a *specie/species* of *fruit/fruits,* not vegetables.
14 Why do we hear so much about *woman's/women's* rights, but nothing about the rights of *children/childs?*
15 Shouldn't you buy *a/some* new pyjamas before going into hospital?
16 Which *are/is* the cheapest *mean/means* of transport?
17 Four *aircraft/aircrafts* took part in the terrorist attack on 11 September 2001.
18 We got *a/some* wonderful *new/news* yesterday. We've won the lottery!
19 The *Swiss/Swisses* have four official languages, don't they?
20 The *outskirt/outskirts* of London *are/is* not very attractive.

4 Road closed

→ SB, Technical reading, p. 136

Look at the text and put the paragraph titles into the right order.

> *A long way off*
> *Collision causes tunnel chaos*
> *Just a lucky coincidence*
> *Not ideal, but ...*
> *Ship ahoy!*
> ~~*Truckers' nightmare*~~

Paragraph 1: _____

Paragraph 2: *Truckers' nightmare* _____

Paragraph 3: _____

Paragraph 4: _____

Paragraph 5: _____

Paragraph 6: _____

1 Thermoplastics and thermosets

→ SB, Text, p 138 Complete the sentences with a word from A (first gap) and from B (second gap).

A	B
advantages	containers
atoms	molecules
heated	non-recyclable
heat-resistant	recyclable
moulded	soft
polymers	suitable
products	temperatures
thermoplastics	thermosets

1 Most polymers comprise hydrogen ___atoms___ bonded to carbon __molecules__ .

2 The two main types of __polymers__ are thermoplastics and __thermosets__ .

3 When __heated__ , thermoplastic polymers become __soft__ and malleable.

4 One of the __advantages__ of thermoplastics is that they are __recyclable__ .

5 As thermosets can only be __moulded__ once, they are __non-recyclable__ .

6 __Thermoplastics__ can only be used at __temperatures__ up to 100 °C.

7 Thermoplastics are ideal for such __products__ as toys, __containers__ and window-frames.

8 Thermosets are quite __heat-resistant__ , so they are __suitable__ for cooking utensils.

2 Vocabulary: uses of polymers

→ SB, Text, p 140 Replace the German words/expressions with their English equivalents from the box.

bulletproof
chemical-resistant
electrical insulators
Impact-resistant
multi-functional
shape-retaining
thermal insulator
weather-resistant

1 Kevlar® polymer lining is used in protective vests because it is (kugelsicher) __bulletproof__ .

2 As polymers are excellent (Elektroisolatoren) __electrical insulator__ , they are used to make many kinds of electrical equipment.

3 The fact that polymer fibrefill is used in sleeping bags shows that it is a good (Wärmeisolator) __thermal insulator__ .

4 If polymers were not (chemisch beständig) __chemical__ , they would not be used to make containers for, say, cleaning agents.

5 Because they are (wetterbeständig) __weather__ , polymers are often used to make garden furniture.

6 The (formbeständigen) __shape__ properties of elastomers make them suitable for stretch jeans, for example.

7 (Schlagfeste) __Impact__ polymers are a good material for everything from car fenders to toys.

8 We say that polymers are (multifunktional) __multi__ because they have so many applications.

3 Blow moulding

Use numbers 1 to 7 to put the sentences into the correct order.

___ At this extrusion stage, the mould is open.

___ A tube of soft, heated plastic is forced through the extruder into a split mould.

5 Compressed air is then led through the air pipe in the centre of the extruder into the hot plastic tube.

___ Finally, the split mould is opened, and the finished bottle drops downwards between the two halves.

___ The force of the compressed air makes the plastic tube expand outwards to the inner walls of the mould.

___ The four drawings show the blow-moulding process, which is the most common way of making plastic bottles.

___ When the plastic tube reaches the bottom of the mould, the two halves close to form the shape of the finished bottle.

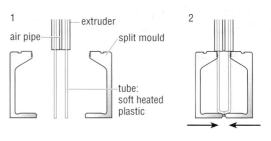

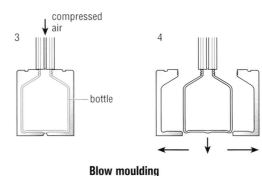

Blow moulding

4 Packaging

Read the infobox and then answer the questions by completing the answers.

Four common polymers used in packaging

PET

(**P**oly**E**thylene **T**erephthalate) is transparent, resilient, light and chemically stable. This makes it very suitable for blow-moulded drink bottles and food containers.

HDPE

(**H**igh **D**ensity **P**oly**E**thylene) is milky white and is used to make bottles and containers for light-sensitive products such as milk, films, cooking oils and many toiletries.

PVC

(**P**oly**V**inyl **C**hloride) is chemical-, heat-and weather-resistant. It is also very stable. In packaging, it is used to make bottles and containers for cleaning agents, disinfectants and solvents (*Lösungen*).

LDPE

(**L**ow **D**ensity **P**oly**E**thylene) is tough, flexible, quite transparent, chemically inert and melts at a relatively low temperature. This makes it the preferred material for all kinds of heat-sealed food packaging, for example frozen food bags and cereal bags.

---

1 *Why is PET used for drink bottles?*

PET is ideal for _____[1] bottles because it is _____[2], so you can see what is in the bottle. As it is _____[3], it is easy to carry and cheap to transport. If you drop the bottle, it won't break because PET is very _____[4]. Finally, the bottle won't react with the contents as it is chemically _____[5].

2 *Why is HDPE particularly suitable for products such as milk and films, for example?*

HDPE is _____[1] so it is often used to protect _____[2] products such as these.

3 *What makes PVC ideal for containers for chemical cleaning agents?*

Cleaning _____[1] are often caustic *(ätzend)*, so _____[2] must be made from a chemical-resistent and very stable material such as _____[3].

4 *What makes LDPE so popular among food manufacturers?*

It is tough and chemically _____[1]. It is also good for _____[2] bags used for _____[3] food because it _____[4] at a low temperature.

1 Hydro-electric power plants

→ SB, Text, p 142 Join a sentence part from list A to one from list B to make true statements.

A	B
1 Hydro-electric power plants convert	a at the foot of the dam to drive a turbine.
2 In mountainous areas, plants are built	b below waterfalls and on fast-flowing rivers.
3 If the water-flow is not strong enough to turn a turbine,	c both relatively cheap and ecologically clean.
4 Artifical lakes called 'reservoirs'	d dams are built across valleys.
5 The energy in the water held back by the dam is	e form behind these dams.
6 This creates a powerful water-flow	f just a useful by-product.
7 The reservoir on the Colorado river was built	g kinetic energy into electrical energy.
8 In the case of the Hoover dam, hydro-electric power is	h released by opening floodgates.
9 The power produced by hydro-electric plants is	i to supply water to Nevada and Arizona.

1 ____ 2 ____ 3 ____ 4 ____ 5 ____ 6 ____ 7 ____ 8 ____ 9 ____

2 Francis water turbine

→ SB, Drawing, p 143 Look at the drawing and complete the sentences with prepositions or adverbs from the box.

> along
> at
> before
> below
> by
> from
> in
> into
> of
> through
> to
> within

1 When the floodgate is open, water flows *from* ____ the reservoir *through* ____ the filter screen ____ the outlet channel ____ the foot ____ the dam.

2 The filter screen stops fish and debris ____ the water ____ damaging the turbine ____ the outlet channel.

3 The water flows ____ the outlet channel ____ the turbine, which transmits the kinetic energy ____ the fast-flowing water ____ the generator, which converts it ____ electrical energy.

4 The electricity produced ____ the generator is transmitted ____ a transformer and then ____ the power grid.

5 After turning the turbine, the water is held ____ a catchment basin ____ flowing ____ the river ____ the dam.

6 A common type ____ turbine used ____ hydro-electric power plants is the Francis water turbine.

7 ____ such a turbine, water is forced ____ the circular turbine casing ____ gravitational pressure and turns a vertical transmission shaft ____ striking turbine blades.

3   Spark plugs

→ SB, Text, p 145 Replace the German labels with their English equivalents from the box.

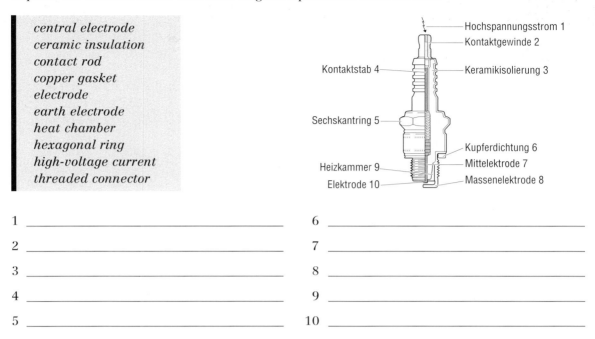

central electrode
ceramic insulation
contact rod
copper gasket
electrode
earth electrode
heat chamber
hexagonal ring
high-voltage current
threaded connector

1 _____

2 _____

3 _____

4 _____

5 _____

6 _____

7 _____

8 _____

9 _____

10 _____

4   Describing the 2-stroke cycle

Complete the description of the power cycle of a 2-stroke engine.

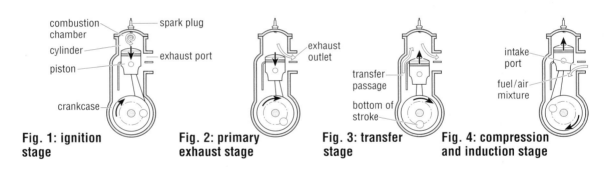

Fig. 1: ignition stage   **Fig. 2: primary exhaust stage**   **Fig. 3: transfer stage**   **Fig. 4: compression and induction stage**

In 2-stroke engines both the combustion chamber and the crankcase take part together in the power cycle. Fig. 1 shows the _____[1] stage. A spark from the _____[2] ignites the fuel/air-mixture, and the expanding gases push the _____[3] downwards. This causes a build-up of pressure in the crankcase. Fig. 2 shows the _____[4] exhaust stage. As it travels downwards, the piston uncovers the exhaust _____[5] so that most of the gases can escape from the _____[6] into the exhaust outlet. _____[7] is the transfer stage. When the piston reaches the bottom of its _____[8], the fuel/air-mixture in the crankcase passes under pressure through the transfer _____[9] into the combustion chamber. There, it pushes the remaining gases out into the _____[10] outlet. Fig. 4 is the compression and _____[11] stage. The fuel/air-mixture is compressed in the combustion _____[12] while the _____[13] port is uncovered to allow more fuel/air-mixture to pass into the _____[14]. Then the spark plug ignites the fuel/air-mixture in the combustion chamber and the cycle begins again.

1

Complete the expressions with **do, go, keep** or **make**.

→ SB, p 146

1 _make_ an effort to lose weight

2 _____ exercises

3 _____ for a run

4 _____ going

5 _____ good progress

6 _____ harm to one's health

7 _____ in shape

8 _____ somewhere by bike

9 _____ sport

10 _____ swimming in the sea

11 _____ use of a fitness machine

12 _____ warm

2 Describing shapes

→ SB, Text, p 147

Describe the form and dimensions of the solid shapes by filling in information from the drawings below.

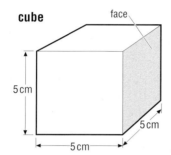

cube face

5 cm

5 cm

5 cm

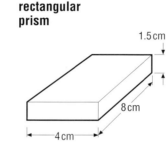

rectangular prism

1.5 cm

8 cm

4 cm

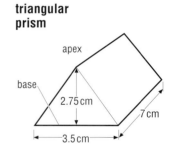

triangular prism

apex

base

2.75 cm

7 cm

3.5 cm

> **How to give dimensions:**
> … **has/have + a +** width/length/depth/height **of** …
> The room **has a** width **of** 3.5 m, **a** length *or* depth **of** 5 m and **a** height **of** 2.2 m.
>
> … **is/are** … wide, … long *or* deep and … high
> The room **is** 3.5 m wide, 5 m long *or* deep and 2.2 m high.

Solid _shapes_ ¹ have a length (end to end) or a depth (front to back), a height (top to bottom) and a width (side to side).

The first shape is a _____ ². Cubes have six sides or _____ ³, all with the same dimensions. The depth, height and _____ ⁴ of the cube is 5 cm.

The next shape is a _____ ⁵ prism. This type of prism also has _____ ⁶ faces, but only the opposite faces have the same _____ ⁷. This prism has a _____ ⁸ of 8 cm, a width of 4 cm and a height of _____ ⁹ cm.

The final shape is a _____ ¹⁰ prism. Triangular prisms have five faces, _____ ¹¹ triangular and three rectangular. The dimensions of the triangular faces are given as a width (length of _____ ¹²) and a height (distance from the centre of the base to the _____ ¹³). This triangular prism is 7 cm long, 3.5 cm wide and 2.75 cm _____ ¹⁴.

3 Exercise bikes

→ SB, Text, p 149

A Fill in an adjective from box A and a noun from box B to make true statements about the exercise bike.

A
> adjustable
> advanced
> easy-to-read
> front
> magnetic
> optional
> ~~robust~~
> silent

B
> ~~construction~~
> display
> extras
> feet
> operation
> resistance system
> saddle
> technology

1 Don't worry. The Stella's

    robust construction

    makes it safe for all users.

2 I bet the touch-pads cost a lot

   – _____

   _____ always do.

3 I think saying the Stella TC is _____ is just silly sales talk.

4 Only the _____ are fitted with castors.

5 The _____ means people of all sizes can use the bike.

6 The computer is fitted with an _____ .

7 The Stella TC has a patented _____ .

8 The sound-proof flywheel casing ensures _____ .

B Link the components on the left with their functions on the right.

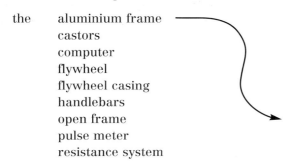

the	aluminium frame	adjust the effort needed to turn the pedals
---	castors	ensures smooth, jerk-free *(ruckfreie)* operation
	computer	gives easy access to the bike
	flywheel	gives the user data on six functions
	flywheel casing	make it easy to push the bike around
	handlebars	measures the user's pulse rate
	open frame	reduces the weight of the bike
	pulse meter	sound-insulates the flywheel
	resistance system	supports the arms and upper body

4 Touring bikes

Use words and expressions from the box to label the drawing of a touring bike.

> brakes
> fork
> frame
> gears
> handlebars
> mudguard
> pedal
> rear light
> reflector
> saddle
> sprocket
> valve

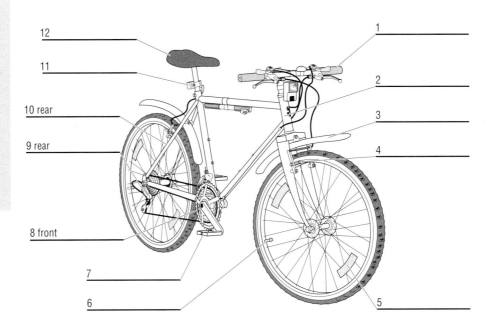

12 _____

11 _____

10 rear _____

9 rear _____

8 front _____

7 _____

6 _____

1 _____

2 _____

3 _____

4 _____

5 _____

1 How CDs work

→ SB, Text, p 150

Say if these statements are true (T), false (F) or you can't say because the information is not in the text (?).

T F ?

1 The pi effect means that the CD spins faster towards the outer edge.

2 The motor spins the CD faster towards the centre than towards the outer edge.

3 The data track comprises bumps and pits.

4 Powerful laser beams can badly damage the human eye.

5 When the beam crosses a flat, the player reads it as a zero.

6 In music CDs, the decoder converts the pattern of 'ones' into an audio signal.

7 Conversion happens at a speed of 65,000 impulses per minute.

8 The bumps form a spiral path from the centre of the CD towards the edge.

9 Most of the output of a CD motor is needed to move the laser reader.

10 The pi effect means that it is easier to pedal a bike with big wheels.

2 Puzzle: CD burners

→ SB, Text, p 153

Solve the clues to find the words and the keyword in the puzzle.

1 The 'C' in 'CD' stand for … .
2 In technical contexts, we usually say … instead of 'nought'.
3 With the label, pre-recorded CDs have four … .
4 You need a special CD … to listen to CDs.
5 Of course CD readers don't damage the e…d data on the data track.
6 CD burners are equipped with both a laser …and a laser writer.
7 Almost all modern PCs are fitted with CD … at the factory.
8 The … of a laser writer is more intense than that of a reader.
9 The laser beam has to be guided along exactly the c… path.
10 'In … with' is short for 'in syncronisation with'.
11 In the text, the more technical word r… is used for 'speed'.
12 Technically, a laser … is just a very powerful laser reader.
13 In laser technology, we usually say e… instead of 'cut'.

3 How a ruby laser works

A Read the infobox and complete the labelling of the two drawings, Fig. 1 and 2.

Protons

Atoms absorb energy in the form of heat, light or electricity. This energy excites the electrons in the atom, making some of them move from a **lower-energy orbit** near the nucleus to a **higher-energy orbit** further away from it (see Fig. 1).

However, excited electrons do not stay in their **excited state,** very long, but soon return to their original **ground state.** When they make this journey, they release energy as a particle of light or **photon** (see Fig. 2).

Lasers organise this rather chaotic process in three ways: 1) the light is **monochromatic,** ie it is of the same wavelength and hence colour; 2) the light is **coherent,** ie the photons move in unison with each other and 3) the light is **directional,** ie it is concentrated in one very intense beam.
A process of **stimulated emission** is necessary to achieve these three properties. A simple **ruby laser** (see below) shows how this is done.

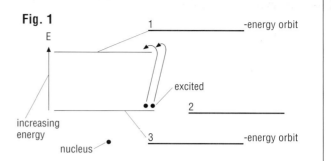

Fig. 1

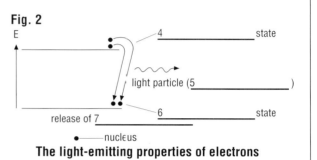

Fig. 2

The light-emitting properties of electrons

B Use numbers from 1 to 5 to link the texts to the drawings.

Fig.1

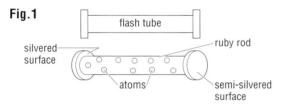

Fig.2

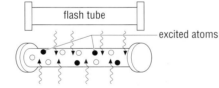

Fig.3

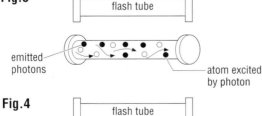

Fig.4

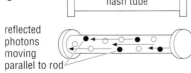

Fig.5

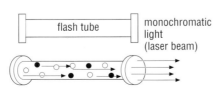

How a ruby laser works

_____ A few of the photons move parallel to the rod so that they are reflected back and forth by the silvered surfaces.

_____ An intense beam of monochromic laser light is emitted from the ruby rod through the semi-silvered end.

_____ Some of the excited atoms emit photons.

_____ The flash tube fires and light penetrates the ruby rod. The light excites the ruby atoms.

_1_ The flash tube is switched off and the laser is inactive.

5 Hybrid cars

■ 1 Hybrid power sources

→ SB, Focus, p 154

Complete the table with a power source from box A and one from box B.

A ~~diesel engine~~ ▪ *4-stroke engine* ▪ *pedal power* ▪ *pedal power* ▪ *oars* ▪ *sunlight* ▪ *thermal currents* ▪ *wind*

B *aero engine* ▪ *electric motor* ▪ ~~electric motor~~ ▪ *electric motor* ▪ *electric motor* ▪ *inboard engine* ▪ *outboard engine* ▪ *2-stroke engine*

hybrid	power sources		
1 diesel-electric bus	*diesel engine*	+	*electric motor*
2 electric bicycle		+	
3 series hybrid car		+	
4 mofa		+	
5 ocean yacht		+	
6 powered glider		+	
7 rowing boat + outboard		+	
8 solar car		+	

■ 2

→ Text, p 154

Use the elements to form the questions that give the answers below. You must add some words. Look at the example first.

Use these abbreviations
FC fuel cell ▪ HV hybrid vehicle ▪ ICE internal combustion engine

1 How long/it + could take/develop/practicable/FC/?

Q: How long *could it take to develop a practicable FC* ?
A: Ten years or longer.

2 Where/you + can find/more information/on/FCs/?

Q: Where _____ ?
A: On pages 174 to 177 of the pupil's book.

3 What/carmakers + do/because/slow development/FCs/?

Q: What _____ ?
A: They are trying to make ICEs more efficient.

4 Why/it + be/difficult/make/ICEs/more efficient/?

Q: Why _____ ?
A: Because they are already near their maximum efficiency.

5 What/other technologies/researchers + work on/moment/?

Q: What _____ ?
A: Developing cleaner fuels and HVs.

3 Components of a hybrid vehicle

→ SB, Drawing, p 155

Link the components on the left to their functions on the right.

1 battery stack	a to carry fuel from the fuel tank to the engine
2 drive wheels	b to connect the battery stack to the motor
3 electric motor	c to keep the batteries charged
4 fuel line	d to power the drive wheels
5 fuel tank	e to power the generator
6 generator	f to propel the car along the road
7 petrol engine	g to store electrical energy for the motor
8 power cable	h to store fuel for the petrol engine
9 transmission unit	i to transmit power to the drive wheels

1 *g*   2 ___   3 ___   4 ___   5 ___   6 ___   7 ___   8 ___   9 ___

4 Parallel and series hybrids

→ SB, Text, p 156

Cross out one word of each pair to make true statements.

1 Series hybrids are *more / less* efficient than parallel hybrids.
2 In series hybrids, the *2-stroke / 4-stroke* engine is connected to the *generator / transmission unit* .
3 Both the motor and the engine can power the *generator / drive wheels* in parallel hybrids.
4 In *parallel / series* hybrids, heat energy from the *brakes / engine* helps to recharge the batteries.
5 Brakes convert *frictional / kinetic* energy into heat energy by applying *friction / heat*.
6 In both *makes / types* of hybrid, a *transfer / transmission* unit connects the power source to the drive wheels.
7 In parallel hybrids, the engine is *always / generally* used to carry *heavier / lighter* loads in *flat / hilly* areas.

5 The cockpit of a car

Use numbers from 1 to 15 to complete the key below.

Key to drawing

___ accelerator pedal	___ fuel gauge	___ mileage indicator
___ air outlet	___ gear lever	___ radio and CD player
11 clutch pedal	___ handbrake lever	___ rev counter
___ direction indicator stick	___ heater and ventilator controls	___ speedometer
___ footbrake pedal	___ light switch	___ steering wheel

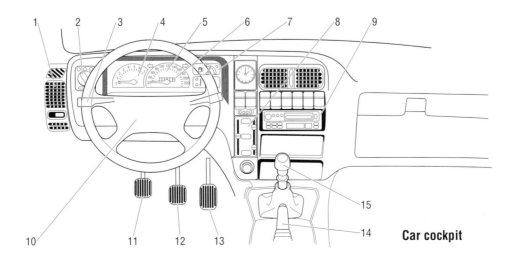

Car cockpit

1 Workshop safety

→ SB, Drawing, p 158

Replace the German words and expressions with their English equivalents from the box.

> *access* ▪ *air circulation* ▪ *daylight* ▪ *extraction fan* ▪ *glass gables* ▪ *is achieved*
> *pedestrians* ▪ *pivot-hung windows* ▪ *rolling door* ▪ *safety measure* ▪ *separate* ▪
> *skylights* ▪ *vehicles* ▪ *windows* ▪ *workshop*

Safety plays a big part in the design of the simple *(Werkstatt)* _workshop_ [1] on page 158. To begin with, there are *(getrennte)* _____ [2] entrances for *(Fußgänger)* _____ [3] and *(Fahrzeuge)* _____ [4], while a ramp and a vertical *(Rolltür)* _____ [5] give forklift trucks, say, free *(Zugang)* _____ [6]. A further *(Sicherheitsmaß-nahme)* _____ [7] is the generous amount of *(Tageslicht)* _____ [8] that can get into the building. This *(wird erreicht)* _____ [9] by means of full-length *(Fenster)* _____ [10] in the side walls, large *(Dachfenster)* _____ [11] in the pitched roof and *(Glasgiebel)* _____ [12] at each end. A third safety measure is efficient ventilation to guarantee good *(Luftumlauf)* _____ [13]. Hence there are *(Kippfenster)* _____ [14] in the side walls, opening sky-lights and an *(Absauggebläse)* _____ [15] in the end walls.

2 Puzzle: a light industrial machine shop

→ SB, Drawing, p 160

Solve the clues to fill in the puzzle frame. Then name the key word.

1 A sealing material given in the infobox is *mineral* granulate.
2 Bad air is removed by an extraction ... .
3 An insulation material in the infobox is p... fibre.
4 Workers are protected against heat, noise etc by i... materials.
5 The supervisor's ... is in a separate cabin.
6 The English equivalent of the German *Wärmeschutzmaterial* is ... .
7 New regulations protect workers against vibrating m... .
8 Even the extraction fan o... on the roof is sound-absorbing.
9 The technical word for 'wetness' is m... .
10 The light industrial building on page 160 has a pitched ... .
11 The technical word for 'shuddering and shaking' is v... .
12 The supervisor's office is fitted with a double-glazed ... .
13 An important insulation material is ... wool.

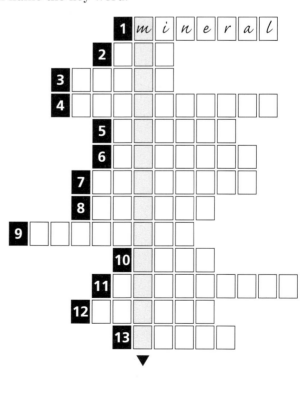

3 The importance of heat insulation

A Complete the text with information from the chart.

The _chart_ [1] shows energy loss in _____ [2] hot water systems between _____ _____ [3] (100%) on the left and net energy output at a _____ _____ [4], ie 48%, on the _____ [5]. What happened to this total energy loss of _____% [6]? Most of the loss, 31%, took place in the _____ [7], which meant that only _____% [8] of the original 100% found its way into the hot water _____ _____ [9]. There, a further energy _____ [10] of 14% led to only _____% [11] of the original energy input actually leaving the tank. Finally, a further loss of _____% [12] occurred in the _____ [13] that connect the tank to the taps, giving a net energy loss of 52% or a net energy _____ [14] at the tap of only 48%.

energy input

31% loss

14% loss

7% loss

100%   boiler   hot water storage tank   pipes

69%   55%   48%

net energy output at hot tap 48%

Energy loss in uninsulated hot water systems

B What has this house-owner done to insulate his property against heat loss and/or frost damage? Complete the key with numbers from the drawing, 1–8.

____ filled cavity between double walls with insulating material

____ fitted double-glazed windows

_8_ fitted sealed door against drafts

____ insulated roof space against heat loss

____ lagged water tank in roof against frost

____ lagged pipe from tank in roof to hot water cylinder against frost

____ lagged pipes from hot water cylinder to taps

____ lagged hot water cylinder against heat loss

Home insulation

Airships – transport in the global village

1 Zeppelins

→ SB, Photo, p 162

Describe the photo of the Zeppelins by crossing out the incorrect or less suitable word or expression in the text below.

The *black and white/colour* [1] photo shows two Zeppelins, which are examples of *rigid/semi-rigid* [2] airships. Such *airships/blimps* [3] attracted a lot of *criticism/interest* [4] in the 1930s as a fast alternative to crossing the Atlantic by *plane/ship* [5]. The Zeppelin in the *background/foreground* [6] is docked at its landing *mast/pole* [7], while the one on the right is *in flight/landing* [8]. A long queue of people seem to be *boarding/waiting to board* [9] the airship, though they may simply be *spectators/technicians* [10], of course. However, the door to the *gigantic/large* [11] passenger cabin below the *balloon/envelope* [12] is open. You can clearly see how the outer *cover/skin* [13] of the envelope has been stretched over the internal *frame/skeleton* [14]. The *floor/ground* [15] at the bottom of the photo is grass as vehicle *paths/tracks* [16] can be seen in the bottom right-hand corner. As there *are no shadows/is no shade* [17], the photo was probably *made/taken* [18] on a cloudy day.

2 Airships

→ SB, Text, p 162

Join a sentence part from list A with one from list B to make true statements about airships.

A	B
1 Airships are classified according to	a above Lakehurst, New Jersey in 1937.
2 Airship technology is an application of	b advertising products above crowded places.
3 Non-rigid airships are often used for	c Archimedes's work on submerged bodies.
4 Non-rigid airships are really	d do not have an internal frame, but a rigid keel.
5 Nowadays, engineers use helium rather than	e hydrogen to give airships lift.
6 Rigid airships like Zeppelins have a fabric skin	f just inflated gas-filled balloons.
7 Semi-rigid airships like the CargoLifter	g stretched over a light metal frame.
8 The Hindenburg exploded	h the construction of their hull.

3 Airship subassemblies

→ SB, Text, p 164

Use the letters a–k to link the subassemblies 1–8 to their functions.
Note that some subassemblies have more than one function, and one function is carried out by more than one subassembly.

1 battens	*b*	a to distribute the weight of cargo etc
2 docking engines	*f*	b to help attach nose cone to envelope
3 forward-propulsion engines	_____	c to improve aerodynamics
4 horizontal fin	_____	d to keep airship horizontal in flight
5 keel	_____	e to move airship forwards in flight
6 landing mast	_____	f to position airship accurately when docking
7 nose cone	_____	g to provide accommodation for crew
8 rudder	_____	h to provide a rigid connection to landing mast
		i to provide fixings for many subassemblies
		j to steer airship in flight
		k to stop airship from flying away after docking

4 Characteristics of modern airships

→ SB, p. 162–165 Use the numbers 1–24 to sort out the characteristics of modern airships and aircraft.

		Airships	Aircraft				Airships	Aircraft
1	cramped *(eng)*		✓	13	poor weight-carriers			
2	do not need runways	✓		14	quiet			
3	eco-friendly			15	relatively easy to fly			
4	fly at low altitudes			16	relatively high construction costs			
5	good weight-carriers			17	relatively low construction costs			
6	harm the environment			18	relatively low fuel consumption			
7	high operating costs			19	relatively spacious *(geräumig)*			
8	low operating costs			20	simple technology			
9	must fly at high altitudes			21	slow			
10	need highly-trained pilots			22	very complex technology			
11	need long runways			23	very fast			
12	noisy			24	very high fuel consumption			

5 How aircraft change direction

Look at the drawings and read the explanatory texts. Then a) label the two missing parts in the first drawing and b) write captions under the four remaining drawings.

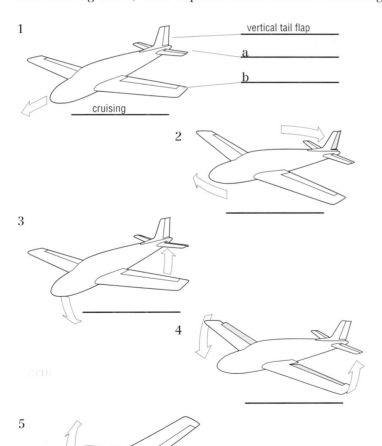

1   vertical tail flap _____

a _____

b _____

cruising _____

2   _____

3   _____

4   _____

5   _____

How aircraft change direction

banking The joystick is used to raise one wing flap and lower the other one. The aircraft banks on its longitudinal axis and flies a curve.

climbing The joystick is pulled backwards towards the pilot, causing the horizontal tail flaps to rise and the aircraft to climb.

cruising All flaps are inactive. The aircraft flies horizontally in a straight line.

diving The joystick is pushed forwards away from the pilot, causing the horizontal tail wings to lower and the aircraft to dive.

flying a curve A footpedal is used to move the vertical tail flap to the left or the right, causing the aircraft to fly in a horizontal curve.

1   Saving water

→ SB, Text, p 167

Complete the water company brochure about saving water with words and expressions from the box.

advice ▪ bath ▪ cars ▪ car-wash ▪ cisterns ▪ consumption ▪ dirty ▪ dishwashers ▪
drinking ▪ dry weather ▪ hose-pipe ▪ instructions ▪ leaking ▪ loaded ▪ low ▪ one ▪
~~shortages~~ ▪ switch ▪ wash ▪ water

WWCS Wessex Water Consumer Services

We live in one of the wettest parts of Europe, yet we still have water _shortages_ [1] after only

two or three weeks of _____ [2]. That's crazy, but what does it mean? Well, it

means one thing for sure: our water _____ [3] is far higher than it should be.

Please help us to go on delivering clean, cheap _____ [4] water whenever and

wherever it's needed by following this _____ [5]:

1 Have a shower instead of filling a _____ [6] because it uses a quarter of the

 water – and ask yourself if a good _____ [7] wouldn't do just as well.

2 Use modern washing machines and _____ [8] with low water consumption –

 and only _____ [9] them on when they are fully _____ [10].

3 Wash your car in a modern _____ [11] plant with _____ [12] water

 consumption – and only when your car is really _____ [13].

4 Fit 'two-stage' toilet _____ [14] – and use 'stage _____' [15] whenever possible.

5 Repair dripping taps and _____ [16] hose-pipes (Schläuche) immediately – and

 only use a _____ [17] when really necessary, and never for washing

 _____ [18].

6 Use modern cooking pots and follow the manufacturer's _____ [19] – most

 people use much more _____ [20] than necessary.

---

2   Word spider

→ SB, Text, p 167

Complete the word spider on page 63 with words and expressions from the box.

cleaning ▪ cooking ▪ drinking ▪ drinking water wastage ▪ flushing toilets ▪
ground water ▪ ~~heating systems~~ ▪ high water consumption ▪ lakes ▪ laundry ▪
personal hygiene ▪ rainfall ▪ rivers ▪ ~~rising demand~~ ▪ sea ▪ showering ▪ ~~springs~~ ▪
washing-up ▪ water shortages ▪ watering plants

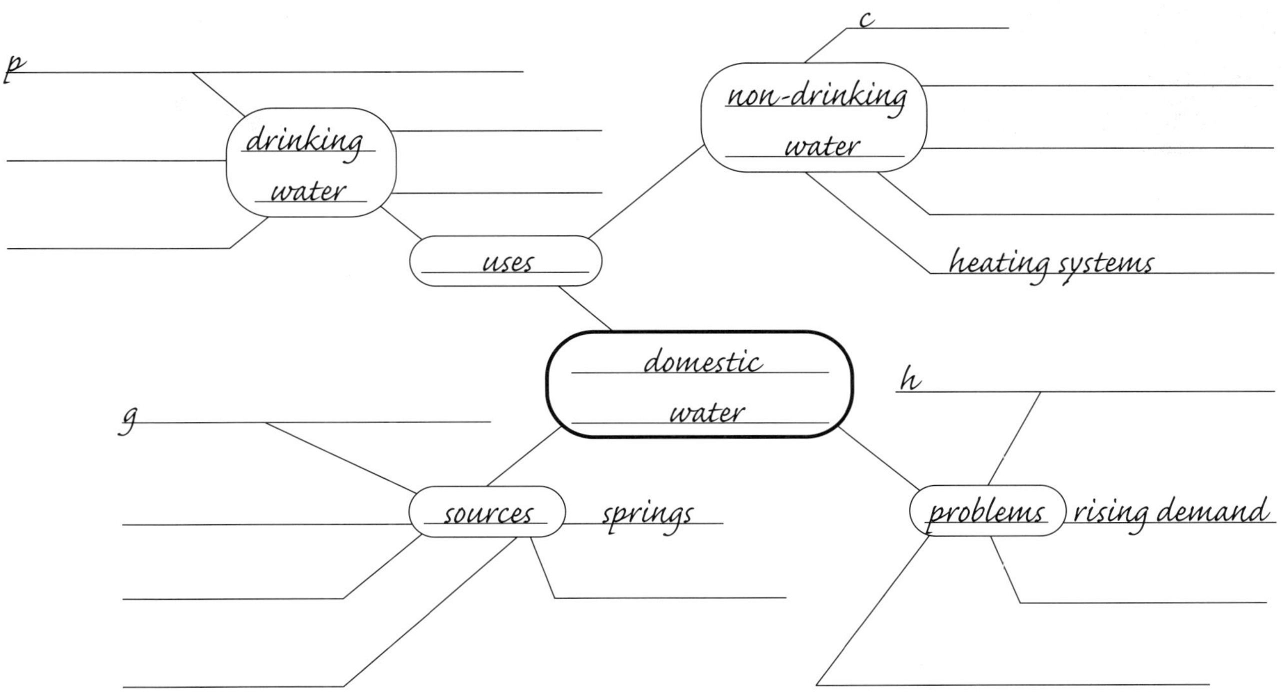
c
p
non-drinking water
drinking water
uses
heating systems
domestic water
h
g
sources
springs
problems
rising demand

3 Rainwater tank

→ SB, Drawing, p 168

Complete the sentences with words from box A (first gap) and one from box B (second gap).

A

access
~~heavy duty~~
inlet valve
outlet pipe
overflow pipe
rainwater
siphon trap

B

cast iron
control unit
excess water
filter
~~seamless~~
self-cleaning
tank

1 The *heavy-duty* tank is made of *seamless* plastic.
2 The ________ hatch is fitted with a ________ cover.
3 The ________ has to pass through a ________ filter to reach the tank.
4 The water ________ is located at the bottom of the tank below the ________ .
5 The ________ connects the tank to the central ________ in the house.
6 The ________ carries ________ and dirty water away from the tank.
7 A ________ stops dirty water from running into the ________ .

4 A rainwater plant

→ SB, Text, p 169

Use the letters a–h to put the sentences into the correct order.

a However, the downpipe is connected to the filter system of the tank.
b If the tank empties, the central control unit switches over to the mains water supply.
c Once the water is in the tank, the control unit pumps it into the house, as needed.
d Rainwater runs off the roof into a downpipe in the normal way.
e The debris in the filter is automatically washed into the overflow pipe.
f The filter system removes all debris from the water before it runs into the tank.
g The filtered water now enters the tank through the water inlet valve.
h This means that water is always available at the outlets in the house.

1 *d* 2 ___ 3 ___ 4 *e* 5 ___ 6 ___ 7 ___ 8 ___

1 Wordfield: crime

→ SB, Text, p 170

Complete the extended word field on crime with verbs from the box.

be
catch
frighten
give
position
prevent
prosecute
record
review
~~track~~

1 to *track*_____ shoppers with video cameras

2 to _____ cameras at strategic points

3 to _____ activity on tape

4 to _____ thieves

5 to _____ thieves away

6 to _____ under surveillance

7 to _____ store activity later

8 to _____ police/courts useful evidence

9 to _____ shoplifters

10 to _____ shoplifting

2 Electronic surveillance systems

→ SB, Text, p 170

Form questions about the underlined parts of the sentences.

1 There are two types of electronic surveillance.

   How many types of electronic surveillance are there _____?

2 Customer surveillance systems work by tracking customers with cameras.

   How _____?

3 Cameras are positioned in parts of the store that staff can't see from the cash desk.

   Where _____?

4 There are usually three or four cameras in an average store.

   _____ in an average store?

5 A reliable surveillance system costs retailers around €3000.

   How much _____ retailers?

6 The basic idea behind simple surveillance systems is to frighten thieves away.

   What _____ behind simple surveillance systems?

7 More advanced surveillance systems record store activity on tape.

   _____?

8 Record-and-review systems are often found in banks and post offices.

   _____?

9 Record-and review systems are not very effective because they are only useful after the event.

   Why _____ very effective?

3 Electronic article surveillance

→ SB, Text, p 172

Replace the German words or expressions in the sentences with their English equivalents from the box.

> *almost certainly* ▪ *electronic tag* ▪ *highly effective* ▪ *local shops* ▪ *loud acoustic signal* ▪ *on sale* ▪ *securely* ▪ *so-called* ▪ *special tool* ▪ *very common*

Electronic article surveillance or EAS is *(höchst wirksam)* _____ [1] because it tracks articles, not people. An *(elektronisches Etikett)* _____

_____ [2] is fixed *(fest)* _____ [3] to all articles *(in Handel)* _____ [4] in the store. When a customer has paid, the tag is removed with a *(Sonderwerkzeug)*

_____ [5]. If the tag has not been removed, a *(lautes akustisches Signal)*

_____ [6] sounds when the article is taken through the EAS gates. A *(sehr weitverbreitetes)* _____ [7] EAS system is the *(sogenanntes)* _____ [8] radio frequency system. This system is the one that you will *(fast sicher)* _____ [9] find in your *(örtlichen Geschäften)*

_____ [10].

4 Surveillance cameras

→ SB, Text, p 172

Complete the sales leaflet with words or expressions from the box.

> *cm*
> *high-performance*
> *illumination*
> *money-back*
> *Price*
> *resolution*
> *same day*
> *shutter*
> *technical*
> *2 years*
> *volts DC*
> *Weight*

Monochrome high-performance surveillance camera

❖ Brief _technical_ [1] description

❖ 1/3 in monochrome _____ [2] imager

❖ 380 line _____ [3]

❖ 0.5 lux minimum _____ [4]

❖ 1/60 – 1/100,000 automatic _____ [5]

❖ 10-14 _____ [6] power requirement

Dimensions: 10.5 × 5.5 × 5 _____ [7]

_____ [8]: 360 g

Guarantee: 2 _____ [9]

Right of return: within 30 days,

_____ [10]

_____ [11]: $49.95

Delivery: _____ [12] dispatch

1 Uses of fuel cells

→ SB, Text, p 174   Use the numbers 1–8 in list A and the letters a–h in list B to join the sentence parts to make true statements.

A	**B**
1 A fuel cell converts hydrogen and oxygen	a according to the type of electrolyte they use.
2 As a rule, fuel cells are categorised	b conventional power plants in electricity-generating.
3 Ecologists and engineers agree that	c for use in household appliances and lighting.
4 Fuel cells also provide a DC voltage that is suitable	d internal combustion engines have some serious disadvantages.
5 Fuel cells could solve the problems	e into electricity and heat.
6 Fully-developed fuel cells will compete with	f of pollution caused by burning fossil fuels.
7 Huge areas of land will still be needed for	g roads and carparks, whatever the power source.
8 The first efficient fuel cell	h was developed by William Grove in 1839.

1 *e*   2 ▢   3 ▢   4 ▢   5 ▢   6 ▢   7 ▢   8 ▢

2 Puzzle

→ SB, Text, p 175   Complete the clues to find the words you need to solve the puzzle.

1 The opposite of 'minimum' is … .
2 The English word for *Fahrzeug* is v… .
3 The adjective form of 'danger' is … .
4 Most cars are powered by internal combustion … .
5 Fuel cells are now a r… alternative to petrol engines
6 In moving vehicles, hydrogen has to be extracted from m… .
7 In its … state, hydrogen is not suitable for use in cars.
8 Spark plugs ignite a mixture of … and air.
9 The adjective form of 'technology' is … .
10 The adjective form of 'to explode' is … .
11 Instable, explosive substances like hydrogen are v… .
12 Anything used to make a product is a m… .
13 Petrol engines are cheaper to make and buy than … engines are.
14 Fuel cells convert … and oxygen into electricity and heat.
15 Early computers and fuel cells were very e… to build.

3 PEM fuel cells

→ SB, Text, p 176

Cross out the incorrect or less suitable word or expression.

The PEM fuel cell is one of the most *hopeful/promising* [1] fuel cell *techniques/technologies* [2]. This *kind/type* [3] of fuel cell could be used both to *power/propel* [4] electric vehicles and mini-power *plants/stations* [5] in homes and offices. In *general/principle* [6], a PEM fuel cell *operates/plays* [7] like a battery except that it never needs *recharging/refilling* [8]. The fuel cell will *generate/make* [9] energy as long as it is *presented/supplied with* [10] a suitable fuel, in the case of PEM cells *genuine/pure* [11] hydrogen. This *solves/works out* [12] the biggest problem with *conventional/ordinary* [13] electric cars, ie the need to *continually/continuously* [14] recharge the batteries. The *chemical/chemistry* [15] reaction within a single fuel cell only generates about 0.7 volts, which is *insufficient/unsatisfactory* [16] for most *applications/jobs* [17]. For this reason, *many/masses of* [18] fuel cells have to be *combined/mixed* [19] in a fuel-cell stack to *grow/increase* [20] the voltage.

4 The parts of a motorbike

Use the labelled drawing of a motorbike to replace the German words and expressions with their English equivalents.

1 Teleskopgabel	*telescopic fork*	12 Kickstarter	_____
2 Lenker	_____	13 Auspuffrohr	_____
3 Vorderrad	_____	14 Zündkerze	_____
4 Kupplungshebel	_____	15 Vergaser	_____
5 Vorderbremshebel	_____	16 Schutzblech	_____
6 Scheibenbremse	_____	17 Blinker	_____
7 Drehgasgriff	_____	18 Bremslicht	_____
8 2-Taktmotor	_____	19 Rücklicht	_____
9 Getriebe	_____	20 Hinterrad	_____
10 Rahmen	_____	21 Hinterradschwinge	_____
11 Kraftstofftank	_____	22 Stoßdämpfer	_____

A 2-stroke motorbike

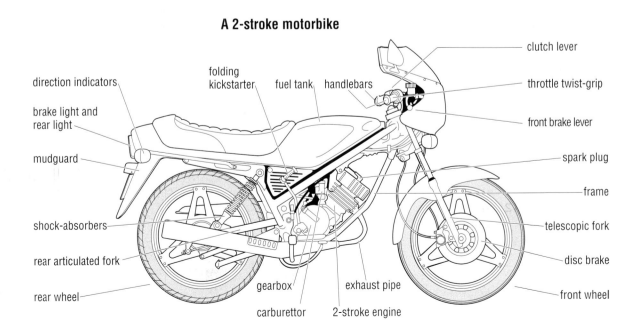

direction indicators, folding kickstarter, fuel tank, handlebars, clutch lever, throttle twist-grip, front brake lever, spark plug, frame, telescopic fork, disc brake, front wheel, brake light and rear light, mudguard, shock-absorbers, rear articulated fork, rear wheel, gearbox, carburettor, 2-stroke engine, exhaust pipe

1 Microwave ovens

→ SB, Text, p 179

Link the components on the left to their functions on the right. Note that two components have two functions.

1 cavity	a to avoid overheating during cooking
2 digital display	b to connect oven to power supply
3 fan	c to generate microwaves
4 feet	d to open door
5 magnetron	e to provide better heat dissipation
6 output regulator	f to provide fan with cool air
7 power cable	g to set cooking time in minutes
8 rectangular button	h to set output of magnetron
9 rotating paddles	i to show the time
10 timer	j to show remaining cooking time
	k to spread microwaves evenly in oven
	l to switch oven on/off

2 How microwave ovens work

→ SB, Drawing, p 180

Complete the description of the path of current within a microwave oven with prepositions from the box.

| at ▪ from ▪ in ▪ into ▪ of ▪ on ▪ through ▪ to |

The current flows _____ [1] the oven _through_ [2] the power cable. It then divides _into_ [3] two paths. The lower path leads _____ [4] the lower interlock switch _____ [5] the door and then _____ [6] the controller. The upper path runs _____ [7] a fuse _____ [8] the back right-hand corner and then _____ [9] a thermal fuse situated _____ [10] the roof space _____ [11] the back _____ [12] the oven. _____ [13] addition, a further thermal fuse is mounted _____ [14] the magnetron. The current then flows _____ [15] the upper interlock switch and controller, where the two paths meet and pass _____ [16] the high-voltage section.

The high-voltage section is made up _____ [17] various components, including a transformer that – _____ [18] Europe – increases the current _____ [19] 230 V _____ [20] 3000 V. The high-voltage current then passes _____ [21] a diode and a capacitor _____ [22] the magnetron, where it is converted _____ [23] radio waves _____ [24] a frequency _____ [25] about 2.45 gigaherz.

3 Echo and Doppler shift

First read the infobox, then go on to read how radar works.

> We have all heard **echos** many times. Shout in the mountains, and your voice will echo back to you. In other words, the sound waves of your voice have detected the mountains around you.
>
> **Doppler shift** is a more complicated. A car comes towards you and the driver blows his horn. As the car gets closer, the horn becomes louder and its note seems to rise. This is because the sound waves are being 'compressed' into an increasingly short time as the car gets nearer. The car passes and the horn becomes quieter and its note seems to fall. The sound waves are being 'expanded' into an increasingly long time as the car moves away from you. This phenomenon is called the 'Doppler shift' after its discoverer, the Austrian physicist Christian Johann Doppler (1803–1853).

Radar (**ra**dio **d**etection **an**d **r**anging) uses radio waves instead of sound waves to make use of echos and Doppler shifts more effectively. This is because – compared with sound waves – high-frequency radio waves can travel much further, cannot be so easily detected and, finally, can be received more clearly even when they are very faint.

Here is an example of how radar is used to detect the position and speed of an aircraft in flight in a air-traffic control system:

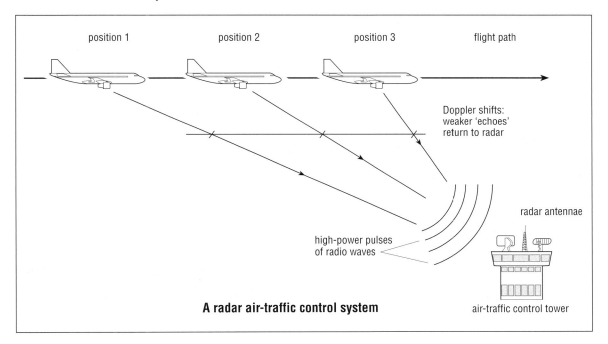

A radar air-traffic control system

Complete the description by crossing out the incorrect or less suitable word or expression.

The ~~diagram~~/*drawing* [1] shows an air-traffic control tower. A radar *antenna*/*mast* [2] is *sending*/*transmitting* [3] short, high-power *beats*/*pulses* [4] of radio waves at a known *frequency*/*speed* [5]. The flight *path*/*route* [6] of an aircraft is *demonstated*/*shown* [7] as it flies over the control tower from left to right. When the radio waves *collide with*/*hit* [8] the aircraft, they '*bounce*'/'*echo*' [9] off it in continuously-changing *points*/*positions* [10]. The same antenna *receives*/*welcomes* [11] the much weaker *return*/*reverse* [12] signals, ie 'echos'.

Because of Doppler shift, the *frequency*/*power* [13] of the return signal appears to *increase*/*strengthen* [14] as the aircraft *approaches*/*arrives at* [15] the tower, and decrease as it moves away. This is because the return waves are being *compressed*/*squeezed* [16] into shorter and shorter periods of time as the aircraft approaches and *expanded*/*stretched* [17] into longer and longer periods as it *disappears*/*moves away* [18]. This *idea*/*phenomenon* [19] enables the *acceleration*/*speed* [20] of the aircraft to be calculated very accurately.

12 Bridges

1 Beam bridges

→ SB, Text, p 182

Fill in a word from box A (first gap) and one from box B (second gap) to make true statements about beam bridges.

A	B
advantage	compression
beam	earth
~~bridges~~	load
concrete	red
exerted	scaffolding
forces	section
foundations	shifting
horizontal	single
tension	supports
upper	~~type~~

1 The first _bridges_ were beam bridges, and they are still the most common _type_ of bridge.

2 In a beam bridge, a _____ beam bends under the weight of the _____ that is crossing it.

3 A bridge with one _____ between two supports is called a '_____ beam bridge'.

4 As the beam bends, the _____ section is subjected to horizontal _____ .

5 During bending, horizontal _____ is created in the lower _____ of the beam.

6 In the drawing, _____ of compression are shown by blue arrows, and forces of tension by _____ ones.

7 The vertical force _____ by the load is transferred to the _____ that hold up the bridge.

8 The supports then transfer the vertical force to the _____ , where it dissipates in the _____ .

9 Most modern beam bridges are built of prestressed _____ using Fritz Leonhardt's timed _____ method.

10 One _____ of this method is that it does not need expensive _____ during building.

2 Wordfield: bridges

→ SB, Text, p 184

Find technical words in the text for these words or expressions of more general meaning.

1 crossing _____

2 legs _____

3 width across _____

4 put under pressure _____

5 (for) getting into them _____

6 flexible _____

7 fixing blocks _____

8 strengthened _____

9 fixed _____

10 road across bridge _____

11 safely fixed _____

12 taken off _____

→ SB, Text, p 184

3 How beam bridges work

The four drawings show the four stages of a simple demonstration of how beam bridges work. Study the drawings and complete the instructions.

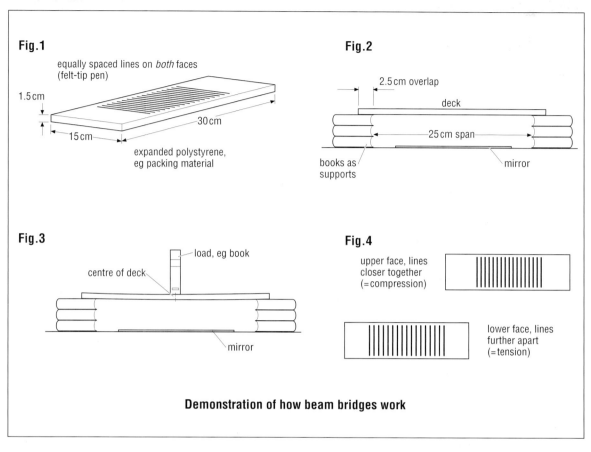

Demonstration of how beam bridges work

To carry out the _demonstration_ [1] you need: 1) a piece of expanded _____ [2], eg packing material, with dimensions of about 30 cm x 15 cm x 1.5 cm., 2) a felt-tip _____ [3], 3) 4 to 8 _____ [4], depending on thickness, 4) a _____ [5] and 5) a fairly heavy object to act as the _____ [6], eg another book.

First, use the felt-tip to draw _____ [7] lines across both _____ [8] of the polystyrene board (s. Fig. 1).

Then make two piles of books as the _____ [9] about 25 cm apart to form the _____ [10] of the bridge. Place the polystyrene board on top of the books as the _____ [11] of the bridge with an _____ [12] of about 2.5 cm at each end. Position a mirror below the 'bridge' as shown (s. Fig. 2).

Now place the load, eg another book, in the _____ [13] of the deck to extert vertical pressure (s. Fig. _____ [14]).

When the load is in place, look at the lines on the _____ [15] face of the polystyrene 'deck'. These will be _____ [16], indicating forces of _____ [17]. Look at the reflection of the lines on the _____ [18] face in the mirror. These will be _____ [19], indicating forces of _____ [20] (s. Fig. 4).

If you can see no difference in the spacing of the lines, then increase the load.

New **Focus on Success Ausgabe Technik Workbook** wurde verfasst von
Michael Macfarlane, Oxford und David Clarke, Witten

Berater/innen (Schülerbuch): Reinhard Ehrke, Flörsheim
                              Philipp Fehrenbach, Leinfelden-Echterdingen
                              Thomas Pache, Euskirchen
                              Dr Gabriele Schneider, Chemnitz
                              Elke Uthoff. Osnabrück

Redaktionelle Leitung: Jim Austin
Redaktionelle Mitarbeit (Workbook): James Abram, Claire Wingfield
Illustrationen: Oxford Designers & Illustrators
Fotos: Titel: Corbis Stock Market: Vasco DaGama Brücke, Lissabon/M. Mastrorillo; action press, Hamburg:
S. 12/Piffel, S. 17/All Action/Jossen, S. 19/Retna Pictures Ltd, S. 43/Rex Features, S. 47; Argus Fotoarchiv,
Hamburg: S. 4/K. Andrews; J. Chipps, London: S. 6; COMSTOCK, Luxemburg: S. 12, 15, 27, 30, 39; Corbis
Stock Market, Düsseldorf: S. 12/J-Y. Ruszniewski/TempSport, S. 21/Strauss/Curtis, S. 24/M. Mastrorillo,
S. 33/L. Lefkowitz, S. 36/R. Lewine/Mug Shots, S. 39/C. Lenars, S. 42/D. Scott; Das Fotoarchiv, Essen:
S. 17/C. Antinozzi, S. 20/R. Oberhäuser/B. Weller; Getty Images: S. 12/D. Noton/Taxi, S. 17/Stone, München:
G. Braasch, S. 18/I. Murphy/Stone; D. Graham, Paris: S. 28; Grundig AG, Nürnberg: S. 12; How Stuff Works,
Inc, USA: S. 23; ORMECON, Hamburg: S. 14

Bildredaktion: Uta Hübner
Umschlaggestaltung: Satzinform, Berlin
Layout und technische Umsetzung: Dirk Risch, Berlin

Erhältlich sind auch:
Schülerbuch
Audio CDs
Schlüssel zum Workbook
Handbuch für den Unterricht

www.cornelsen.de

Dieses Werk berücksichtigt die Regeln der reformierten Rechtschreibung
und Zeichensetzung.

1. Auflage, 3. Druck 2007 / 06

© 2003 Cornelsen Verlag, Berlin

Druck: CS-Druck CornelsenStürtz, Berlin

ISBN 978-3-464-06182-4

 Inhalt gedruckt auf säurefreiem Papier aus nachhaltiger Forstwirtschaft.